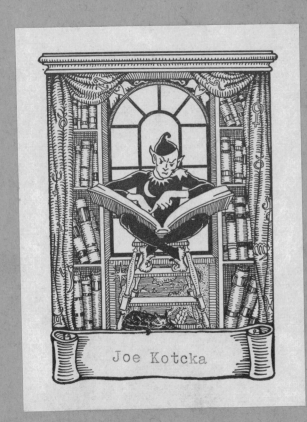

Joe Kotcka

On Thin Ice

Henry Jelinek, Jr.
and Ann Pinchot

On Thin Ice

PRENTICE-HALL, Inc.,
Englewood Cliffs, N.J.

On Thin Ice by Henry Jelinek, Jr. and Ann Pinchot

To the parents of the five Jelineks.

"Who can find a virtuous woman? for her price is far above rubies.

"Her children rise up, and call her blessed; her husband also, and he praiseth her."

Proverbs: Chapter 31: 10 and 28

"As arrows are in the hand of a mighty man; so are the children of the youth.

"Happy is the man that hath his quiver full of them."

Psalm 127: 4 and 5.

chapter one

My BROTHER, OTTO, DARK, WIRY, INTENSE, IS wondering how Maria is doing.

My sister, Maria, fair, willowy, serious, is wondering how Otto is doing.

They aren't scared. Yet they have a right to be uneasy and aware of possible personal danger. Years of discipline, however, have schooled them to restrain their emotions. Although they occupy separate dressing rooms, they keep themselves busy by ticking off details of immediate concern to them—the condition of the ice in the stadium; how the character and ideology of the judges may influence the final scoring; the perils involved in their presence here in Prague, perils that have no bearing on their extraordinary skating talents. No, it isn't fear. But they are nevertheless gravely sensitive to the extraordinary circumstances that have brought them here. And since they are both so young—Otto is twenty-two and Maria two and a half years his junior—and since their childhood in Czechoslovakia was saturated with terror and destruction, the potential threat cannot be ignored. It shows itself in the dryness of their lips, in the white glint of their eyeballs, in the acceleration of their heart beat.

Otto and Maria have come back to Prague, the city of their birth, and long ago the scene of idyllic happiness as well as tragedy, to compete in the World Figure Skating Pairs Championships. Naturally gifted and magnificently trained, they have flown the Atlantic from their new home in Canada on a mission greater than their personal needs. They have in their favor the "X" factor, that miraculous spiritual quality stoking their hearts and will. Yet, they wonder—and with due concern since this is a Communist dominated land—whether their skill and dedication will be enough.

In this month of March 1962, the art of skating occupies the limelight in Prague. Today, skaters from democratic countries are present in person. They can be seen; they can be admired, perhaps even touched, by any Czech citizen who has a ticket to the vast new sports hall or who is willing to trudge to the International Hotel, where all the young competitors are quartered.

The 1962 World Figure Skating Championships are a fabulous hit in Prague, a complete sellout every night, with disappointed thousands crowding outside the arena and small groups gathered around every television set in the country. All forms of sport and athletic entertainment are immensely popular in the Communist countries, perhaps because they represent to the downtrodden an escape from dreary regimentation. No matter how a skater or hockey player must bend to political authority, he is nevertheless an individual on his own, once the starting signal is sounded. He stands or falls then strictly on his own merits. He is gloriously free. An athletic competition is a kind of freedom that is denied the average Communist citizen. Next to participating in a contest, the best thing is to be able to watch the performance and enjoy a touch of freedom vicariously.

My brother and sister symbolize liberty to the Czech people. For Otto and Maria were originally Czech citizens, who fled their homeland fourteen years ago, when it adopted Communism. To the subjugated people, they are visible proof that the Iron Curtain philosophy is a grotesque lie. For it is evident to Prague that Otto and Maria Jelinek have not been corrupted by the Capitalistic west. Indeed, they are ideal specimens of young humanity —friendly, attractive, modest, cultured and tremendously skillful. How can one, therefore, put credence in the philosophy of the People's Republic when it is so evident to all that these two youngsters are better athletes and finer human beings for having escaped the regime? If they do win the championship, it will indeed be a glorious strike for the principles of democracy.

These are the vital issues at stake in Prague today. Not only the personal ambitions of my brother and sister are involved; not only the dreams of my parents, but the hopes of millions of subjugated Czechs, who are identifying themselves with Otto and Maria Jelinek.

Therefore, as Otto sits in the stuffy little dressing room under the Winter Stadium, he knows that the return of the Jelineks to Prague is the major story of the day. The Red press has referred to him and Maria only as members of the Canadian team. There is no mention of their fantastic background. It doesn't matter. The people know; the mysterious underground has transmitted the truth to the Communist-plagued populace. Not even the Jelineks' impressive performance recently at a Swiss skating show, which was televised on the European network and transmitted to Czechoslovakia, created this kind of reaction. At the moment, Prague, proud of the inspiring Jelinek saga, has become one vast dedicated cheering section for the two valiant young expatriates.

Being aware of this situation doesn't help the state of Otto's nerves. Since he and Maria are the focus of thousands of prayers and good wishes, Otto tries to disengage his mind from the spiritual and ideological challenges involved in the competition. He stares at the blank wall opposite him. He concentrates on his skating boots. To lace up a boot is such an awkward procedure. You might say, Otto reflects, that my heart is right down there with my heels.

Less than an hour to wait. When the hands of the clock finally signal the moment, he and Maria will emerge on the ice to participate in the exhibition that is the climax of a decade of discipline, hardships and dreams. This is the World Figure Skating Championship, a competition acknowledged by the foremost skaters as the toughest test of all. Here one builds up to the apex of talent, skill and sportsmanship. But as Otto and Maria will go through their intricate performance, as the bleachers will resound with cheers, everyone in the Stadium will be conscious of the political interplay that is part of the drama. In the background is the Goliath of Communism, ruthless and inhuman; in the spotlight, a couple of youngsters who are the object of bitter and vindictive hate of the Red officials. The Communist dictators have neither pity nor tolerance for defectors.

So Otto glumly laces his skating boots and stares at the blank wall opposite him and then, all at once, it grows into a living panorama, a movie of the mind, with all family memories blown up to life size and the shadowy figures of the poignant and excruciating past marching by like ghosts.

The film freezes abruptly in his mind and the image of our mother comes vividly alive to him. Our mother is herself a skillful skater and accomplished sportswoman, but more importantly, the motivating force behind the scenes, the nourishing source of patience, fortitude and a simple love of God that has been our inspiration. Hers is the magic glue that has kept us together, five strongly stubborn individuals—her children—and our patriarchal father. She has fused us by love and faith into a close knit and devoted unit.

That our mother and father dared not come to Prague to watch first hand the World Championships for which they had worked and prayed is one of the ironic whims of our destiny. They are in Davos, Switzerland, on the Jakobshorn, a peak, 11,000 feet high, where they have been informed the television transmissions would provide clear viewing.

It is not often that we are divided, for our family is known for its togetherness. But Otto recalls the time once before, at a crucial moment in our lives, when our family had been cruelly divided. Our father and our oldest brother, Frank, were out of Czechoslovakia. To my father's anguish, he was compelled to wait outside the border of his country, wondering whether my mother and the four younger children would succeed in their flight to the border.

Yet at this tense moment, Otto does not feel entirely alone. Their coach, Bruce Hyland, is with them, as well as their dear friend, Jim Proudfoot. Jim is a top Toronto sports writer, who has accompanied Otto and Maria to Prague. It was to Jim that our mother gave her final pleading injunction, "Jim, I beg of you. Don't let my children out of your sight in Prague."

It was a promise that Jim was to keep faithfully.

Otto is usually desperate for time; between school and practice and competitions, the clock seems to play tricks on him, and he often wishes twenty-four hours would stretch to forty-eight. But presently, he is annoyed with the laggard ticking of the clock. There are still thirty minutes to wait until he and Maria are due on the ice. Thirty minutes, Otto thinks, and a montage freezes the film in his mind. Thirty minutes have a traumatic meaning for him—indeed for all of us Jelineks. We associate it with the day long ago, when here in Prague, the Gestapo telephoned our father at our home and announced: "We are coming to fetch you. You have exactly thirty minutes."

Across the dressing room corridor, Maria is having a bad time with her bootlaces, but the fretting is an incidental mask for her inner qualms. What are she and Otto doing here in a Communist stronghold? Their parents, their brothers, all of them barely escaped with their lives from Prague, yet she and Otto have had the temerity to return, to flaunt their skills in the face of their enemies. Would they be allowed to compete fairly? Would they be given safe conduct out of the country as promised? Dared one accept the grudging Red concessions in good faith? If anything were to happen to them, how would their mother accept it—she who had already had the full measure of suffering? Perhaps it had been a mistake; perhaps it was an exercise in foolish vanity on their parts and a misguided dream on their father's. One small family even backed by a democratic government does not defy the People's Republic, to whom a promise is merely an expedient.

Her fingers are clumsy in tying the laces. This slowness has often earned her a brotherly rebuke, but never on the ice. She wonders if the blades are too finely sharpened; she fusses with her hair; she frets about her trim-cut royal blue costume with a white mink collar. Finally, she wanders into Otto's dressing room, ostensibly to talk, privately for the kind of comfort their togetherness often gives her.

Otto is combing his hair. Otto is combing his hair energetically. This is the third time in as many minutes that Otto is using the comb, and she understands that it is a meaningless gesture to occupy his hands. He manages a tepid smile. He looks down at his boots.

"The next time I unlace these, I shall be world champion—or..."

"Or..." Maria begins, and her voice fades.

Fifteen minutes to the deadline.

Otto thinks: Fifteen minutes after the Gestapo telephoned our father, in that previous awful time, the police were starting the long drive from Baron Petschek's old palace up the winding Hradcany hill. And our father was saying goodbye to us and telling us to be brave and look after our mother. Are there times when bravery is a misnomer for foolhardiness? Our father had inspired us all with his own courage. Although his attitude had brought him to the edge of death, he had not once deviated from his standards. This was the reason for our presence today in Prague. This was our destiny from the first time our Canadian teacher put us on public display as wobbly little Robin Redbreasts.

The quick rap on the door makes Otto jump. But it is nobody as fearsome as the Gestapo—only that handsome lovable tyrant of a coach, Bruce Hyland, himself a former Canadian ice dance champion. For all his laconic exterior, Bruce is perhaps the most nervous of the trio.

"Time to go, kids. Margret Goebl and Franz Ningel are just about to come off the ice. I want you to know those Germans skated real well."

A pause. Bruce repeats for emphasis, "Yes, they skated real well." This is painfully obvious, for only superb skaters are competing today.

Otto goes back to combing his hair. A senseless repetitious gesture, yet Maria, loyal and sympathetic, looks at him as though it were a gesture really worthy of attention.

She turns to Bruce, "Is *my* hair all right?"

"Just fine," the coach agrees. Were Maria in pigtails or in a bouffant hairdo, it would have been all the same to Bruce. He flips a quick glance at his watch. He takes a deep breath.

"Okay, kids. Let's go."

"Let's go," Otto echoes, being second in command.

Maria murmurs, "If only the butterflies would stop fluttering in my tummy."

The three walk out to the arena, just as Goebl and Ningel, to ringing applause, are leaving.

"Good luck," says the little German girl, kissing Maria's cheek. Otto shakes the hand of her partner, Franz Ningel. Then, my brother and sister hear their names announced. Maria is startled to hear the announcer speak in Czech. But, *of course,* they are in Czechoslovakia, and although Canada has been their home for many years, Czech is still the family language of the clan. It is nevertheless strange to hear the mother tongue in this now unfamiliar setting.

"Easy now," Otto says softly to Maria, whose disturbed though unspoken thoughts are known at once to him. Such is the coincidence of their thinking that strangers often assume my brother and sister are twins.

"Easy now," Otto repeats, this time in English.

"I'm all right," Maria replies in Czech.

"Good luck!" someone booms in English. "Skate well, you two, so I have something really worthwhile to write about."

It is the voice of their friend, Jim Proudfoot.

"Thanks for your good wishes," they reply. But it would have been better had he kept quiet. For Jim, their adored companion and admiring fan, is also their jinx. Almost invariably when he is on the sidelines during one of their performances, they are apt to tumble. The last time it happened was the previous year in Philadelphia, and it was a tragic accident, not only for the physical injuries involved, but also for the fact that it occurred the day before the North American Championships. The doctor who attended them insisted it would be "sheer madness" for them to compete. But compete they did, since our family has been conditioned to the concept that the impossible takes only a little more determination and grit. Now, here is dear exasperating Jim reminding Maria and Otto that he will be watching them.

Coach Bruce, who thinks of everything, suggests, "A drink of water before you take off, kids?"

"No, thanks, Bruce."

Otto is reasoning fiercely with himself: Now look, boy. What's all the fuss about? Five minutes on the ice. Just five minutes of skating, that's all there is to it. Haven't we perfected the necessary quality and style in ten years of preparation?

The last thought is particularly upsetting. Ten years! Ten years of preparation, of sacrifice, of sweat and of dreams—and in five minutes they would know whether they measured up to the expectations of their parents, their coach, and more explicitly, the millions of emotionally displaced compatriots, for whom they were a symbol of the Free World.

Not a moment left for brooding.

They are "on." The crowd in the arena hails them with an avalanche of joyous greetings.

"Wave," says Maria, for once giving the orders. Otto obeys. He says from the fullness of his heart, "They're our people—and they're totally on our side."

Our people. There is a magnetic flow between audience and performers, a subtle message that dispenses with mere words. Our people. Our flesh and blood—and now they are slaves. We must do our best—for them.

Nearly 19,000 pairs of hands clap a thunderous ovation. If the results of the World Figure Skating Pairs Competition depended on the audience, Bruce Hyland reflects, there's no doubt of the winners. But added to the multitude are nine judges. Eight of them are stern, hardfaced men, and the one woman judge is no less righteous. They are as tough and uncompromising, Bruce knows, as any judge of the Czechoslovak People's Republic dealing with economic saboteurs and illegal border-crossers.

Bruce squeezes Maria's arm; this is their private goodluck signal.

Then, hand in hand, striking in their simple costumes, Otto and Maria move silently to the start-spot in the center of the arena.

The most crucial moments in life involve both tears and laughter.

The laughter of our parents is polite and constrained, as they move close to the television set. An estimated audience of 150,-000,000 people are watching as my brother and sister glide into the initial stages of the competition. Our parents are among them, not in the Prague Stadium, but high over Davos in the Inn at Jakobshorn. The Inn, snug in its womb of deep thick snow, is open daily from ten in the morning to four in the afternoon, at which time the last tram descends to Davos. Our parents have arranged to stay at the Inn, since the transmission of the televised events will best be seen there. Together with our parents, George Hasler, an old friend and Secretary General of the International Skating Union, and his charming wife, make up a congenial if solitary quartet. They are surrounded by a staff of twenty-two servants and rescue boys, all equally intent on the small television screen. The royal attention given our parents doesn't ease their tension.

Father, to make small talk, speaks of the cost in energy, time and money devoted to shaping a possible future champion.

"In skating, there are many talented young people who have never made a great name because of outside circumstances," he says in his deep husky voice. "If you come from a family that is too rich, you're not likely to acquire the necessary iron discipline. If you're too poor, you cannot afford the expense of training."

He takes a sip of the Liebfraumilch. "Nobody has ever become a world champion without skating around the world." Our father has his unique way of explaining cold mathematical facts. "That is 25,000 miles. Now you figure that each mile costs about two dollars. That makes a total of $50,000 which must be spent to make a skater ready for the Championships. This is the estimate of Gus Lussi, who was Dick Button's teacher and who eventually became the summer coach of Otto and Maria for many years.

"This, remember, is the cost for one champion.

"We Jelineks are blessed with two. It takes a lot of cork to underwrite such a gigantic long range project."

Cork has been the Jelinek family's bread, butter and Liebfraumilch for three generations.

Our mother—as she confessed later—had her ears blocked to Father's efforts to keep her from worrying. Maria has inherited the outer serenity of our mother. But inwardly mother is intense, and when such a mood grips her, she often shreds a paper napkin, or plays with a bit of paper, a habit Maria has unconsciously imitated. Father saw our mother fussing with a napkin, and then he heard her cry of anguish as Maria went down.

Meanwhile, at the Stadium at Prague, in the rink-side pressbox, Jim Proudfoot shuffles uneasily in his seat.

Dick Button and Jim MacKay, his colleague, tune up mentally for the comments they will soon be sending on the ABC television *Wide World of Sports* program.

Otto and Maria push off. They quickly pick up speed in rhythm with the vigorous pulsating music of Bedrich Smetana, to whose Czech melodies they have skated all during their competitive trials. In many North American cities, they have introduced

Smetana and Dvorak to new and appreciative audiences. Today, in the Prague Stadium, every fan feels the familiar surge of its beat in his own heart, as Otto and Maria continue weaving their way by miraculously swift turns and loops to the very apex of their performance.

Otto is absolute master of the situation. Here it comes, he thinks as he and Maria get into position for their lifts and leaps. This is a usual reaction for him. In ending the jump that is the prelude to each hoist, his arm muscles flex, his hands seek his sister's in a close firm grip, so that, as his own spring from the ice loses its thrust, he is able to continue the hoisting process.

In one unforgettable moment, worthy of casting into marble statuary, the music brings Maria sailing supremely high over Otto's head, one knee tight bent, so the line from her leg to her foot becomes a base, supporting a breath-taking upsoaring feminine curve. The following musical note sends her arm stretched out, parallel to that base, until the hand arrests it, leaving the index finger extended in a characteristic little gesture, pointing forward and upward in aspiration. Thus, a touch of ballet completes an evolution that began with split-second timing; a mechanical precision that is firmly founded on the straight line Otto's skates make on the ice.

By now the butterflies that have been plaguing Maria have departed. Usually they leave when she is nearest the stadium roof, as she is completing the double turn above her brother's head, while he glides swiftly over the ice.

Abundant confidence is theirs. The importance of the occasion is forgotten; they are fused into one beautifully precise human mechanism, both swimming simultaneously, with a shared spirit and a single mind. Now Otto steers Maria to the next move.

Dick Button, in his television comments, is infected by the atmosphere of excitement in the stadium. "Each skater will do a double Axel jump, which consists of two and a half revolutions," he announces. "This is so difficult, it is done only in solo skating. Now, watch this coming up, double Axels by *both* skaters."

Maria, her lovely proficiency giving its own message to the judges, springs once more into the air. She thinks, Please, oh, please, dear God, let me land this jump. Prayers have replaced the threat of more butterflies. Otto is performing superbly. His smile comes from within and reflects supreme confidence in his ability and training. You sure got that one okay, Otto boy, he tells himself. But the smile abruptly freezes in horror. Maria has landed awkwardly. She has failed to keep her footing.

There is a gasp in the audience. Dick Button, scarcely able to control his shock, reports, "Oh, Maria—she's fallen! It was a very difficult move, though."

Maria is down. She slides across the unyielding ice for a foot on the hand and knee that only a moment ago contributed to the perfection of her pose. She is down just long enough for the humiliation of her fall to flicker across the world's screens. But she knows, as does Otto, that one more such mishap—a mishap from which no skater is immune—and their dreams of winning the title will plummet to earth. For them, there can be no second chance. They know it. Everyone in the inner circle knows it. It was a moment of the most shattering anguish.

In Davos, our parents are stunned.

"They've had it." Father's voice is despondent. "They can't win now."

Mother stares at the television screen in silence. We Jelineks don't like to lose. Father has taught us that the wish is father to the deed only when the wish is accompanied by work and belief. Failure has never disheartened him for long. "One more step," Father has always affirmed, "and failure often turns to victory."

Mother is now shredding her fine linen handkerchief, the only indication of the state of her nerves. It is her children who have just suffered an excruciating humiliation in plain view of millions of stadium and television watchers. She longs to be with them, to comfort them. Usually, it is Otto who reassures her. Before an examination at school, before a test of skating skill, he says, "Don't worry, Mother. It will be—somehow." Otto, the young Pan of her four sons—charming, unruly, competitive, a complex young man whom it is impossible to censor or discipline. And Maria, her only daughter, so exact, so honest, such a dear honorable little person. She bleeds for them in silence.

She watches Father pour himself a whisky. He has switched drinks and added too much water, a sure indication of anxiety. But neither of them will dissolve in self-pity or pity for their

children. They have survived through God-given courage, and
that faith will not forsake them now.

I am the jinx, Jim Proudfoot thinks, seated unhappily in the
stadium pressbox.

Sometimes those who love us the most can be bad for us; we
try too hard to please them, and this tensing up can trigger disaster. This seems to be the case with Otto and Maria. They adore
Jim, but invariably when he is in the audience, one or the other
will take a tumble. Therefore, even at the risk of being scooped
by his colleagues, he deliberately turns his back on the ice. It is a
tremendous sacrifice for him, both as friend and reporter, for the
only way he can follow their progress now is to watch the reactions
of the spectators.

Meanwhile, only Otto and Maria appear to maintain their
phenomenal poise. The tumble shook them, but the aftermath is
typical—they are more determined than ever to win. They go
through the remainder of their performance with verve, zest and
perfection that filled the hearts of viewers with breathless awe.

Nevertheless, Otto is thinking, One more mistake—one small
mistake—and we're lost.

It is characteristic of Otto that he says "We." No technical
error on his part had brought Maria low. He hadn't faulted in any
lift. Yet the mistake was nonetheless dual, an error of the partner-
ship. Not that Otto was being chivalrous. It was simply that he
and Maria are so thoroughly welded into a team, so perfect in
their unison, that it would be unthinkable for either to blame the
other for a mishap.

The judges' eyes are eagle sharp.

Coach Bruce fights the sickness in the pit of his stomach.

Now Jim MacKay takes the microphone from Dick Button.
"Maria and Otto move back into their usual routine, still giving
the impression of complete confidence. The Jelineks have been
planning for years just for this appearance. When they left Czechoslovakia, Otto was eight years old and Maria was six. Now they
are twenty-two and not quite nineteen. They returned to Prague
last year, as you may remember, but the championship contest was
cancelled. So they decided to skate on for another year in order
to come back for this great occasion."

Working together all these years has developed the extrasensory perception in Maria and Otto, and it was this sense that saved them after Maria's tumble. They made a decision simultaneously, but without direct verbal communication to each other. This decision was to change the sequence of their program. They omitted part of a spin—a "sit" spin, the success of which would have counted for a good deal in the final markings. The change, however, meant that they could give themselves a couple of seconds of grace for readjustment.

Another lift, now. A more complex one. Its end brings Maria, legs extended in a magnificent wide-angled inverted V, above Otto's head. His long powerful arms extend their full length, holding her high. Then, as quick as mercury, he throws her higher still. After one instant of immobility, gravity brings her gracefully to the ice. Otto brakes the lower stage of the descent gently; his sure grasp meets hers and allows her to glide slowly to a new start position at his side.

That throw is a sensation.

"Just look at Maria leaving Otto's arms," Dick Button says with the appreciation of one superb artist for another. "It does not seem that her fall has hurt their performance so far."

The five minutes allotted to each pair of skaters is fleeing by. Except for the fall, everything is going perfectly for them. Otto skates like a man inspired; Maria in her feminine grace, matches his inspiration.

Jim MacKay reports with scarcely concealed admiration, "Brother and sister look almost exactly alike. They are almost exactly the same size. They are still skating as if they are held together by an elastic band, staying the same distance apart, moving in, moving out. The pair are the center of attraction here in Prague, returning to the city of their birth. Big crowds have been turning out just to see them at practice sessions at the Winter Stadium."

Otto displays an ease and polish that conceals beautifully the immense effort that has gone into perfecting his technique. Then, in the midst of their performance, he begins to worry about the condition of his skates. Perhaps it had been unwise to have them sharpened, he thinks, after feeling something out of the ordinary as he takes off on a jump—some tiny impediment that immeasurably retarded the take-off, robbing it of the purity of absolute perfection.

Now Dick Button is reporting: "Here's another unique move coming up, a 'death spiral.' Watch Otto now. An Axel from a front spiral—and he catches Maria as she falls into a backward arch, which is the 'death spiral.' "

As she goes into the "death spiral," Maria's head sinks slowly backwards toward the treacherous ice. This part of the act is a Jelinek specialty. Otto begins the move with a fantastic leap and a turn in the air, which brings him down at the exact spot where Maria can place her hand in his. Thus, their arms are linked in a descending plane and only one boot saves her from falling prone on the ice. It skims around in a wide circle whose center and fulcrum are focused on Otto's spinning skate. To complete the rapidly revolving clockwork, Maria's free foot, high in the air, goes round and round to match the motions of Otto's free outstretched arm.

The speed of the spin increases. Down, down goes Maria's head, her spine again arched, the back of her head no more than an inch above the ice. Her hair caresses its glittering surface, a caress so gentle that her hair-do is seldom disturbed.

The "death spiral" is finished.

Perfect, Otto thinks. It worked perfectly.

His glance meets Maria's radiant smile. All is going well with us, Otto, isn't it so? she seems to be saying. The smile is a private signal between brother and sister. It usually shows itself when she is executing the overhead cartwheel. A simple cartwheel, ankles over hands, such as urchins often perform for tourist coins. But Maria is no urchin. She achieves a display of exquisite perfection, her hands on Otto's shoulders, her long lovely legs flailing the air above.

They are on the home stretch.

The home stretch has thousands of exuberant fans in the stadium clapping with enthusiasm. Their thunderous rhythm keeps time with the Dvorak melody as Maria and Otto cross the ice in a reversing step. One instant they seem to be one, both facing in the same direction. The following moment, they are going backwards, and then forward again. With each change of direction, Maria's skirt swirls about her hips, in a bright and insouciant display.

"Two more lifts," Otto whispers. All has gone well for them except for the beastly fall. The Dvorak music comes in, the movement slower, quieter, and again Otto encourages Maria, but more fiercely now, so his words are both a prayer and a dedication. "Make them good, kid."

Again Dick Button is reporting, "Two overhead lifts, but done in opposite directions. Here comes the first overhead . . . The same, now, again, but in the other direction . . . Beautifully done!"

One glorious flourish of rising skates in the end leap and for the Jelinek "twins" it is over.

"Finished," says Maria, totally happy now.

Otto gives her hand a quick squeeze. This is in lieu of saying, "Just great, kid." The cheering grows in volume like the swelling of organ music. They acknowledge the plaudits with the grace that is part of their flawless style and good manners. Otto bows deeply; Maria does a curtsey, scraping back her left skate as she descends on the other knee with a zest that makes a flowering ruffle of her brief skirt.

The bow and curtsey are repeated to the judges. They spin around and salute the other tiers of the stadium. Then they glide off the ice.

The Jelinek contribution to skating history has been made. The family's entire saga, triumphs and tragedies, was telescoped into those five minutes.

Amid the tumult of the continuous applause for these two young Canadians who are also Czech, the crowd cannot fail to mark the rapid heaving of their chests. This sight more effectively than words demonstrates the terrific effort that has gone into their five minute battle with gravity and ice.

They are still breathless when Dick Button, elbowing to the barrier as they leave the rink, puts his microphone in front of them. But they are empty of words as well as of breath. Bruce helps them out, giving them casual questions that can be answered briefly, to allow them to come back to normal.

Dick asks: "How do you feel about your performance? It was magnificent in my opinion."

He wants Otto to face the U.S. television equipment. But Otto, knowing that our parents are watching from the Swiss network, turns to the Swiss cameras. Between gulps of air, he says, "Thank you very much, Dick. Let's hope the marks are good."

"Are you happy with the way you skated?" Dick asks.

"Yes, except for one minor . . ."

"I would like to say that you are to be congratulated on not letting a fall bother you and picking up and going on to give such a magnificent performance."

"Thank you." Otto's chest pains him less now.

Dick Button asks what they think of the reception given to them by the Czech audience. Otto is polite, but withdrawn. The fans couldn't have been kinder; he and Maria are deeply moved and most grateful. His eyes, however, are on the judges who will shortly announce the marks for the Jelinek performance.

"I don't think they stopped applauding through your entire number," Dick says with a broad smile. He is interrupted then as the judges raise the boards showing the large white score figures.

The stadium is hushed for a long breath.

Then Dick says with excitement, "Tremendous marks! Are you happy with them, Maria?"

"I suppose so," says Maria. She sounds not too convinced.

Otto says, "We're happy with them right now. But we'll have to see what comes next. The competition isn't over yet."

Indeed not. The formidable Russian pair, Ludmila Belousova and Oleg Protopopov have still to perform. The Russians skate a near flawless routine. Their scores are extremely close to those of Maria and Otto. Trainer Bruce tries desperately to figure out the final standing. He rechecks the scores, but always the Russian pair seem to come out in first place. Finally, he pushes his way into Otto's dressing room, which is always crowded with Jelinek admirers.

Jim Proudfoot is with Otto. "I just figured it out. You came in first."

Bruce shakes his head. "I don't think so, Jim. The Russians seem to have a higher score. But I can't be sure."

Now it is the moment when the top competitors and their retinue of trainers are summoned from the dressing rooms to the arena. Maria recalls little of that dramatic moment. She remembers only thinking that her fall must have hurt their chances. All that Otto remembers of that fateful walk past the competitors barrier to the open arena is the awful pounding of his heart, as though he had experienced another five minutes of excruciating loops and leaps. Nevertheless, he manages a weak smile for his Russian rival. Bruce is pressing Maria's arm; the secret uplifting signal between coach and beloved pupil. Maria maintains an outer poise, that admirable poise that is the envy of her contemporaries. But the butterflies she had left near the ceiling in one of their magnificent leaps are again playing leap frog in her stomach.

Now the victory fanfares sound out. Audience and competitors feel the tightening of nerves, the goosebumps on the flesh, the long unending moment before a voice breaks the tense silence.

Then it comes. The deep voice over the loudspeaker is giving the results of the Pairs Figure Skating Championship of the World.

chapter two

SOMETIMES ONE OF MY BROTHERS—FRANK OR Richard or Otto—makes a bad joke about the family tendency to tumble on ice.

It all began when our father literally fell at our mother's feet. The incident took place on a frozen pond. It laid low an elegant young man who until that moment had been gliding over the ice with superb style and confidence. His tumble aroused the amusement of a girl standing with her parents on the bank of the pond. Just before the mishap occurred, her parents had been waving to the young man, beckoning him to join them.

The girl's name was Jara and she had come here to toboggan. She was enchantingly lovely. But her laughter was a child's. Her mother scolded her.

"Who is he anyway?" Jara asked, feeling that the rebuke was out of proportion to the incident. After all, a fall invariably aroused good-natured laughter in bystanders.

Her father replied, "A young friend of mine. He and the Baron came up yesterday from Brno to hunt with us."

The young man, no longer elegant and unruffled, his male ego somewhat shaken by the fall, joined them. But not before Jara's father, in a stern aside, cautioned her to control her amusement. He would not allow his friend to be humiliated.

The man who chided his daughter was to become my grandfather.

The young man who was red with embarrassment was destined to be our father, Henry J. Jelinek. And Jara, of course, our mother.

My grandfather was a lawyer, a man of reason and logic. The legal profession is rarely given to second sight. But I have often speculated whether that morning in Moravia, he had an inkling that these two young people were destined for each other.

Perhaps, there was something in their chemistry, a subtle attraction, that was evident to those about them. The setting was as romantic as a fairy tale; the crystal lustre of mountain peaks in the sun, the bracing air that whipped color into fair skins, the brilliant costumes of the skaters. Years later, when we were children, Mother often told us the story of their first encounter, and once she added with a shy smile, "You may not believe me, but that morning while we were waiting for the train to take us to Rozinka, where we were to skate, I had the feeling that something special was going to happen that day."

Jara's intuition may have been inherited from her grandfather, a beloved judge who had a deep insight into the complexities of human nature. Or it may have come from an earlier ancestor, one of the great men in the history of the Czech nation—the Hussite general, Jan Zizka Trocnova. But fortunately, the veil of the future protected the young romantics.

It was not Jara's parents who actually introduced Henry to their daughter, but a close friend of Henry's, Baron Amand. The young baron, who had a hunting lodge in Rozinka, had shared many escapades with Henry. He was present at the pond and suggested that the three of them go tobogganing. Amand was well aware of the fact that Henry, who was a gay young blade and characteristic of his time and place, was much more interested in attractive Madame Zizkova than in her inexperienced young daughter, Jara. It was fashionable for a young man to pay homage to a handsome mature woman. But the baron was astute, too, and no doubt he saw the spark of interest in Henry's eyes as they gazed on Jara. He heard the subtle plea in Henry's voice, asking, "Miss Jara, might I be allowed the pleasure of helping you pull your sled?"

So Henry hauled the sled, and Jara trotted beside him up the slope speckled with Sunday tobogganers. Their conversation was banal. Did you have a pleasant Christmas? Isn't the air bracing? Do you enjoy winter sports?

The landscape was all dazzling crystal under a fresh snowfall that softened the rugged outline of the hills and laid its lovely white burden on the branches of the trees. The sun cast shadows as they walked through the deep snow, oddly silent and shy.

Suddenly, Jara deserted Henry.

"Here we are!" she shouted, dashing up to the crest of the hill with surprising agility. Her parents who had lagged behind looked at her in astonishment. Henry, himself in superb physical condition, was impressed. Here was a mercurial nymph in her skating costume, seventeen, slim with an exquisite profile, and a profusion of ginger-colored hair framing her delicate face. Henry, experienced and discerning at twenty-seven, found himself drawn to her.

"I think I'll wait here," Jara's father said. He handed the second sled to her mother, and said with a smile to Henry, "My friend, don't let them tire you out. The women of my family have magnificent but exhausting energy."

Precisely then, as though to emphasize her father's statement, Jara set off alone on her toboggan. She called over her shoulder to Henry. "You can go with Mother."

By the time Henry had piloted Madame Zizkova to the end of the run, Jara was already halfway up the hill again. Although his attentions had been claimed originally by the enchanting, sophisticated mother, Henry was exasperated with her pert, elusive daughter. He was not accustomed to young girls who played games with him on their terms.

"I must go," he said to Madame Zizkova. "Or I shall miss my train. Please say goodbye to Miss Jara."

Madame Zizkova suggested that he might like to join the family for New Year's. There was to be a party at the village inn.

"I'm afraid not," Henry said. "I must be back in Brno. I've already promised my friends there that we will see 1928 in together."

"I am sorry also," Jara's mother said. "The New Year's Eve parties in Rozinka are really quite famous. I am sure you would enjoy yourself."

Henry nodded, gallant but noncommittal, and then with a gay salute, he was gone.

Next day was the last of 1927. The sun shone over the village but an icy wind roaring down from the hills pushed the thermometer below zero. Jara, bundled in furs, tendrils of her ginger-colored hair curling out of her white cap, was driving in a sleigh to meet her aunt, who was arriving by train for the party. She was startled by the jingle of bells from a sleigh approaching from the opposite direction. Suddenly, in the front seat beside the driver, she spied Henry. His dark humorous face was beaming with delight at her astonishment.

"Good morning, Miss Jara," he said casually, "a bit blustery for tobogganing, don't you think?"

"Why, yes—so it is," Jara managed to answer and then Henry drove by, with the gay salute that was characteristic of him. Now, what on earth was he doing in Rozinka, she wondered, after he had announced his departure for Brno?

Her aunt's chatter, as they drove from the station, was inconsequential and demanded no answer. Jara was musing about the young man. Perhaps he had decided to accept her mother's invitation. It was no doubt foolish of her to be so pleased over the prospect of his appearance tonight. I'll ignore him, she resolved. He is much too sure of himself.

When Jara and her parents arrived at the *Bily Kun*—The White Horse Inn—the place was already alive with song and laughter. On the dance floor, young couples in native costume were twirling in a lively Czech mazurka. On the dais at the far end of the room, the village musicians were plucking at their instruments with more will than discretion but their occasional false chords only regaled the guests.

Henry was at a large table not yet filled; his lively anecdotes evidently inspired his fellow guests with hilarity. Jara spotted him instantly but pretended to be unaware of his presence. Her casual air cut no ice with this knowledgeable young gallant. He spun around and beckoned to the Zizka family.

"Good evening! I've saved seats for you."

The Zizkas and the aunt joined him. But Jara had already been claimed by an attractive young man in a green uniform, who escorted her to the dance floor. Once the dance was ended, the young man brought her to the table where Henry, in the midst of a fresh anecdote, ignored her. Jara was offended by his lack of attention, so she turned to her neighbor and began chattering in a lively fashion. Henry was outraged; he paused and looking directly at her, declared, "Look here, either you keep quiet—or I leave."

His ultimatum, born perhaps of the stirring of jealousy, shocked the table. But the situation was saved by the sound of the painted old clock. Long before it struck the twelfth note, the guests had jumped up from the table, linking their arms, kissing each other and shouting, "Stastny novy rok. Happy New Year!"

Again and again, wine glasses were replenished as toasts were drunk to the New Year.

It was a gay company, merry and uninhibited, with the joy of living that found earthy expression in food, wine and good companions. And none was gayer than the village priest of Rozinka. He was a big jolly man, the picture of health, high spirits and a belief that God put the good things of life on earth for man to enjoy. He was a picture of his convictions, his jowls well fleshed from rich Czech pork, his belly ample as the ale barrel that was the source of its girth. He shouted for attention in a voice commensurate with his vast bulk.

"Hear, all of you! I shall now choose a couple at random and show you how a wedding ceremony is performed."

His announcement didn't shock the guests; the mood was spiked with wine and hilarity. Gazing around the room, the priest spied Jara. He beckoned to her. As she stepped forward, the young man in the bright green uniform wanted to join her. But the priest waved him grandly away. Again, he scanned the revellers. "You there—you come with her!"

He was pointing to Henry.

Henry pretended to be diffident. But the dancers, amused by this impromptu match-making, gently shoved him toward the bar. The mock marriage began to the bridal march from *Lohengrin*. But there was nothing sacrilegious in this ceremony; it was all in good fun, and highly amusing, even down to the musicians' sour notes. Jara was swept along in the fantasy of the moment. But later, all of the Zizka family wondered if Henry, that adroit and witty young man, had arranged it with the priest, or whether the priest, even in his cups, had had a sudden flash of premonition.

The real wedding didn't take place until three years later.

Only those who lived in Czechoslovakia in the days before World War II can place credence in its fairylike atmosphere. It was a Hollywood musical brought to life, a world of baroque elegance and beautiful women and gallant uniformed men, a world passionately dedicated to its new independence but never allowing its rich cultivated tastes to be adulterated by politics.

So the wedding of my parents was a major creation, requiring the skill of caterers, dressmakers, florists, jewelers and all the attendants essential for such a grand production. Among the guests were captains, colonels and at least one general. Father, a captain in the cavalry reserves, was in his parade uniform, blue tunic, red trousers tucked into high black patent leather boots. As the young couple left the church after the ceremony, the bride radiant in white satin and heirloom lace, they walked through an arch of flashing sabres.

They expected naturally to live happily ever after.

That is, as happily as the future, loaded with the perils of Nazidom and Communism, would permit.

We young Jelineks were raised in a sprawling town house. It is consistent with the culture of the Czech background that our parents should have taken up residence in an ancient stone mansion whose windows afforded its residents a wide sweep of the Old Town. The street door opened to a passageway leading to magnificent gardens. The main entrance led to a sweeping staircase that was designed as a showcase for beautiful women in elegant gowns and men in uniform and blazing decorations. There were crystal chandeliers and great stone fireplaces, a magnificent library, vaulted ceilings and parquetry floors. The house was a labyrinth of hallways, vast bedrooms, pantries, an enormous kitchen, root and wine cellars and a playroom and gymnasium which Father had constructed for future generations. The house was a symbol of the pre-war splendor of Prague society, and our mother, although young and somewhat naive, was trained by her own background to fulfill the role of a distinguished young matron.

She loved Prague. A romantic girl, cushioned in the downy aura of the classics in poetry and music, she found the city a harvest for her eyes and senses. The enchantment of Prague was hers to ex-

plore—the turrets and spires and golden domes; the noble bridges
and the intriguing little alleys where craftsmen practiced their
arts, the cobbled squares, the cafes with soft lights and romantic
music, the parties in ancient mansions where string quartets played
Mozart in the musicians' galleries, and the wide space of the city,
protected by its seven hills. She loved it all and with the flesh and
blood of her body, she transmitted that passionate, inspired love to
all of her children.

My American and Canadian friends, who have been guests in
our home outside of Toronto, often tell us, partly in admiration,
partly in awe, that our father reminds them of Mr. Day, the
patriarch in the play, *Life with Father*. Father is perhaps a Czech
version of Clarence Day, gruff on the outside, tender within.

But none of our North American friends has seen the father of
our childhood—the fierce, agile, punctilious man who bore the
weight of his responsibilities with stoic endurance and extraordinary grace. True, he is in the image of the Victorian *paterfamilias*,
and sometimes his faith in his own wisdom is wearing for his
children, who are determined that if they must profit by mistakes,
those mistakes should be *theirs*. But it is he who has kept us a
family through the most excruciating trials. He can be tough with
us; he often is. But each of his five children has discovered a soft
spot in his formidable armor. This is particularly true of his only
daughter. Maria's technique is on a par with a diplomat's. "Please,"
she coaxes Father, wanting her way in perhaps some impractical
matter.

"No!" Father thunders. "I will not hear of it!"

Maria is smarter than her brothers who joust head on with
Father. Maria, for all her tomboy ways, has our mother's feminine
wisdom. She lets the matter ride; she looks injured and woebegone.
Father offers to buy her a pacifier—a new frock, a fur jacket, a ski
parka. No; Maria declines. She droops until Father is riddled with
self guilt. Then, like a soft enchanting kitten, she pounces. By
now, a week has passed, and again she presents her request. Father
growls—and gives in.

The Jelinek fortune in Czechoslovakia was built on the cork
industry. Cork is used not only for wine- and champagne-stoppers,

but for many other practical products in industry. With the Jelineks, the enterprise was no shirtsleeves to shirtsleeves affair in three generations. Father loved life, but he was intrinsically a business man with visions that placed him ahead of his time. He had tremendous knowledge of the family business; finances were therefore no problem for the young couple.

Father insists he married Mother on one condition—twelve sons. Eleven to make up a soccer team, one as a reserve in case of sickness or injury to the others. But this avowed aim of creating the Jelinek Eleven received a shattering setback after Maria was born. Mother had started out to fulfill his hopes; her first three children were sons—Frank, Richard and Otto. But then Maria broke the chain and by the time I was born, Father was reconciled to the compromise Nature had imposed upon his plans. Nevertheless, he remained a vigorous sports enthusiast.

During World War I, Father was a cavalry cadet at the Austrian Military Academy and head of his class in equitation. After the war, in the heady first days of Czech independence, he kept up his interest in riding and participated in many a steeplechase. He rode with unabated zest but seldom won.

After their marriage, Father took Mother riding every morning, sunshine or rain. He was eager to have her become an expert horsewoman. The stories of her experiences are part of our childhood memories.

"One Saturday afternoon while my instructor was plying me with advice," Mother used to tell us, "your father listened with growing impatience. The trouble was that the instructor was much too polite. He treated me as if I were a piece of precious crystal on top of the horse. 'If you please, Mrs. Jelinek, sit up straight . . . If you please, Mrs. Jelinek, point your toes *up.*' I listened, but all the while, my position in the saddle remained unchanged. Suddenly, your father who was leaning against the wooden fence around the training ring, lost patience. He leaped the fence easily and landed in the ring. He grabbed the whip from the instructor's hand and exclaimed brusquely, 'Now, my dear, this is where *I* take over.' With that, he lashed the horse until the animal broke into a furious gallop. As we whirled around the ring, your father cracked the whip again and again to make the horse gallop even faster. I held on desperately but finally I lost my grip. I took a tumble, and after picking myself up out of the dirt, I rushed to our house, packed a suitcase and took the first train home to mother. Your father telephoned, he telegraphed, but not once admitting he was wrong, you understand. This was to him a logical way to learn to sit a horse well. His pleas didn't soften my injured pride. Only when he came to fetch me, loaded down with flowers, candy and a shy confession that life without me was unthinkable, did I weaken. After all, I adored him. So the following morning, we were out on horseback again. Together. And from that day on, I received countless compliments on my beautiful riding."

As we children grew old enough to sit a horse, we also received lessons. Not from Father but from a more disciplined teacher than Mother's original master.

Mother was during the early years of her marriage a dedicated sportswoman. She was active in the Czech SOKOL movement, a world renowned gymnastic organization dedicated to the credo "A sound mind in a healthy body." The English translation of Sokol is falcon, the fierce and proud bird. A hundred years ago, the Czechs—within the Austrian-Hungarian monarchy—organized the Sokol, and at exactly the same time, the American Czechs founded a Sokol-U.S.A. unit. When the Communists took over Czechoslovakia in 1948, they liquidated the organization. However, to thousands of Czechs, it was heartwarming to discover that on February 15, 1965, the Postmaster General of the United States issued a five cent stamp, commemorating the centennial of the founding of Sokol.

At any rate, all of us were conditioned from infancy to participate in sports. I understand Mother often carried each of us by the ankles, our heads dangling upside down. The neighbors never got accustomed to the sight.

Father was not gentle with us either. As a matter of fact, his training methods were more rigorous. Holding a child by the arm and leg, he would spin the little one above his head, or throw him into the air a dozen times. The purpose was to strengthen the young muscles. But while these rigorous exercises were taking place in the nursery, Mother would crouch nervously out of the path of the flying missiles, meanwhile crossing her fingers for luck.

While there were only two children—Frank and Richard—our

parents took them each winter to a mountain resort on the German border. Here the two boys, who were still under school age, would ski from Christmas to Easter. Father was occupied with the cork factory in Prague during the week, but each weekend, he came to visit his family.

This one Saturday, he did not make an appearance.

Mother was not too concerned, thinking the urgency of a business matter had kept him in Prague. She was untroubled by rumors of political crisis; as a matter of fact, politics were during that period unimportant in her way of life. So she took the boys on their customary daily walk. However, this morning, they passed a large group of soldiers resting by the road. Mother was puzzled, for according to their uniforms the men were German. Armed with curiosity and courage, she addressed the nearest officer. "Whatever are you doing here?" she asked him in his own language.

"We are on our way to Prague," he answered.

He smiled and Mother, thinking it was a joke, smiled with him. But then he added, "Seriously, madam, we are on our way to occupy Prague."

On the way to occupy Prague? Did this mean that the Hitler Germany was taking over, in peacetime, the Czech's capital city? It was impossible! Yet for all its improbability, Mother suddenly grew cold with anxiety.

"What should I do?" she asked, putting the question more to herself than to the German. "My husband is in Prague. Ought I to dash back there?"

The German officer was respectful and polite, as Germans usually are, when people don't interfere with their plans. "Why not stay here and see what happens?" he suggested.

He added it would not be wise for her to hazard the trip to Prague. In view of the circumstances, there was nothing she could do but heed his advice.

So hers was a little sidelight on the tragic history of her country. For in Prague, citizens were gathering in sorrowful groups to watch the alien Panzers roar in.

This was the fateful and gloomy March 15, 1939, the day Czechoslovakia was effectively occupied by Hitler's army. This was the Führer's ruthless followup to the bloodless victory, six months earlier, in the Sudeten provinces. The loss of these provinces destroyed the country's power to defend her borders. Now, in addition, Czechoslovakia lost its most precious treasure—its freedom.

Europe, that day in March, was less than six months away from total war.

Overnight, our nation's way of life changed completely. For our people, the Wehrmacht invasion was an endless nightmare. Thousands of innocents were imprisoned. Medieval torture was revived. Citizens were degraded. The Germans dissolved the Czech army and air force.

No family remained unaffected by the terror.

Uncle Jan, Mother's brother and a cavalry major, was ordered to surrender his arms and his horse. He considered his horse, a black giant of a charger named Abuki, his best friend. When the young German officer arrived to claim the animal, he saw Uncle Jan patting Abuki in sorrowful farewell.

"Don't be angry with me," the German pleaded. "I know how you feel. But I have my orders."

Jan strode away, his eyes moist. Whenever, in later years, Mother told us children the story, the tragedy never failed to move us deeply.

But compared to what was ahead for us, it was a small matter. In spite of uncertainty and ordeal, life somehow continued. Much was changed; much remained. Lilac bloomed in the lovely hillside gardens of Prague. Our family continued its existence in what dignity and force it could muster.

Athletics became a source of release for anxiety and frustration. The Germans had confiscated all horses except those used on farms, so riding was now impossible. The Germans restricted all travel, so skiing was also out of the question. Ice skating became the all-embracing Jelinek sport. Grandfather Zizka had been manager of the Czechoslovak National Exhibition and in this capacity had been responsible for the construction of the first ice stadium in Prague. My parents skated at the arena. So did Otto, Maria and myself, as tots, since we were all born during the German occupation.

It was during this period of national and family subjugation that our parents first had their dream of seeing some of their children compete in the Winter Olympic Games. Mother was especially attracted to ice skating because it involved so many human emotions, because of its suspense and its exquisite blending of athletics and ballet.

Frank, being the eldest, was singled out for the family dream. He was put on skates and entrusted to an excellent instructor. To Mother's disappointment, he showed little enthusiasm for the sport. Since he was basically a fighter, hockey had greater appeal for him. Once on the ice, he would watch a hockey game, longing to participate. Finally, during one practice session in figure skating, Frank fell and broke his leg. The accident ended his skating career.

But Mother wasn't giving up. Richard was singled out next. As soon as he grew into Frank's skates, he was out on the ice. But he too preferred hockey to figure eights, so once again, Mother was forced to look for fresh material.

It was during this period that Otto, aged six, and Maria, four, were put on skates for the first time. Their early attempts were made without the benefit of a coach. They simply tried to copy the glides of the older skaters.

One day, after a frustrating workout with our older brother, the instructor turned to Mother. There was such reluctance and embarrassment in his manner that Mother said helpfully, "You wish to tell me that my son, Richard, has no talent for figure skating."

"Oh, he has talent, all right. What he lacks is interest. I'm afraid, Mrs. Jelinek, that it is a waste of your money and my time."

The instructor paused and gazed at the crowded ice. "You see those two little ones?" he asked. "They have both talent and interest."

Mother followed the direction of his hand. "But those are also my children," she said, watching Otto and Maria, happily absorbed in cutting scraggy figure eights. "Let us concentrate on them."

The trainer was delighted with this happy discovery. "They have something, those two. You will see, Mrs. Jelinek. One day, I shall make a pair of champions out of them."

It was not in his destiny to realize the fruition of his dream. But he taught the children as long as it was possible, even waiving his fee when Mother admitted the Communists had confiscated all the Jelinek possessions. But it was a dream that nourished Mother through the times of crisis.

*   *   *   *   *

chapter three

THE TELEPHONE RANG. IN PRAGUE, DURING THE Nazi rule, a knock on the door in the night or an unexpected telephone call were enough to arouse terror.

Father lifted the receiver, "Yes?"

"Good morning, Mr. Jelinek. This is the Geheime Staats Polizei speaking." The voice was as soft as a German guttural voice could be; the Gestapo knew when to be sentimental. "We should like to congratulate you on the birth of your son. Now, be ready in half an hour."

"Oh." Father felt suddenly quite helpless. Only several hours before, a friend of the family had taken Mother to the maternity clinic. Toward morning, Father had slipped into an uneasy sleep, and now it was the cold buttermilk dawn of another grim dreary day for him. The elation that accompanied the news of the birth of his other sons and his daughter was lacking. Because the new arrival spelled a kind of doom for him. They know about my son's birth before I do, he thought bitterly. Their spies are even located in the maternity clinic.

The call made it urgent to write Mother immediately. Finally, Father penned a note characteristic in its brevity, keeping his emotions restrained. He had not quite finished when the telephone rang again; this time Doctor Jerie was calling with official news of my arrival.

"Congratulations, sir! You have a ten pound son, and he and your wife are both doing well."

Father thanked the doctor. Then he added soberly, "I have some disturbing news, Doctor, and I would be grateful if you told it to my wife as tactfully as possible. I am writing to her but she may not get the letter. The Gestapo is taking me inside."

After a lengthy pause, the doctor asked, "You don't even have time to see your wife before you—go away?"

"I'm afraid not."

"Well, goodbye, sir." And the doctor added in a low voice as though he were afraid of being overheard, "And may God be with you."

Perhaps the word Gestapo has little significance to the generation that has grown up since World War II. But during its time, the name aroused a shudder in one's heart. It was the abbreviation for the *Geheime Staats Polizei* (Secret State Police) and it ruled the occupied countries with a sadistic inhuman power that left a river of bloody sadism and suffering in its wake. To those of us who lived under Nazi domination, Gestapo was a dreaded word spoken only in a whisper.

The Gestapo first took an interest in Father shortly after the crown-cork factories in the German Reich had been blown up under the British and American bombing raids. Prague, a city beautiful enough to merit immunity and preservation, escaped the bombings. This left the Jelinek stopper factory the only one intact. It was doomed, therefore, to become a vital segment in the Nazis' war machine.

From Gestapo headquarters in Berlin came an order that our factory was to be seized and converted into German defense operations. In order to justify the take-over, the Nazis accused Father of participating in a conspiracy against them. They said he organized political meetings in our home. In wartime Czechoslovakia, many innocent citizens were shot for less.

Of course Father was a plotter against the Nazis; so were thousands of other Czechs. But the accusation of his holding secret "political" meetings in Mother's drawing room was too stupid even to be taken seriously. Nevertheless, it was a moment of grave peril for all the Jelineks. The ice was thin.

A fortnight before Mother was scheduled to go to the clinic to await my birth, the Gestapo came to arrest Father. He pleaded with them to wait until after Mother's accouchement.

"It could go badly with my wife were she to have the sudden shock of hearing I had been taken away," he said.

Whereupon he made his sole pact with the enemy. He bribed them. They agreed to leave him be, in return for his promise not to leave the house under any circumstances. In accordance with their orders, he pretended to be indisposed, staying in at home under "voluntary" house arrest, while waiting for his child to be born. Mother suspected something was amiss, but Father proved to be a good actor. He dared not share too much of his thoughts with her during this crisis, for fear that his manner would betray him.

My parents were hoping that I would arrive on October 28th, the Czechoslovak National Day, which would have permitted some slight celebration. To mark October 28th for its own sake would have been counted as a capital crime by the Nazis.

However, perhaps because of the tension that was a natural climate for my family in those days, I made my appearance four days early, October 24, 1944. Accordingly, shortly after my birth, the Gestapo was on the wire with Father to remind him of their pact.

"Now—be ready in half an hour," the curt voice had informed him. The Gestapo's show of reasonableness had ended. The receiver shut off the harsh summons with a bang.

Thirty minutes left of a life. For once the Nazis arrested him, there was little likelihood that Father could count on a future. Thirty minutes to settle his affairs, make some semblance of order to protect his wife and family, bid his children farewell. The letter to Mother was written. Father packed a few garments in a small bag. Now there was but fifteen minutes left. He hurried through the chill shadowy corridor to the nursery where he found Anna, the nurse; he soothed her fears and asked her to look carefully after the children until Mother returned from the clinic. Anna could scarcely control herself; tears were spattering her cheeks as she rushed into the kitchen to prepare a package of food for Father to take with him. Little was said. Father, no doubt, longed to load her with instructions and warnings, but instinct forbade it. He must not burden her. Anna would need all her self-control to handle the children and give them some kind of security.

A peremptory knock on the front door reminded him abruptly of his perilous situation. He went downstairs. He opened the door. The Gestapo commissars faced him, one with a heavy rifle over his shoulder.

The older one asked brusquely, "You ready, mister?"

"I am ready," Father said. "But first, may I go and say goodbye to my children?"

"All right. Five minutes." From his guard's tone, it was evident to Father that the claws under the surface civility were being unsheathed. Feeling somewhat like a character in a Kafka dream, Father returned upstairs, the two men at his heels, and turned into the nursery. Anna had raised the shades, for the Jelinek children were early risers. Father bent over Maria's crib and kissed her. He was aware of the baby fragrance, the soft touch of her plump cheeks, the flush of recent sleep that bathed her skin with a rosy glow.

"Be a good girl," he whispered.

Maria gurgled sleepily in response.

In the adjacent room, Frank was reading a story to Otto and Richard, who although wide awake were still under their covers. The sight of his sons made Father tremble, not for himself but for them. If any harm were to come to him, what would their future be? How could Jara fend for them and herself? He recalled the day in Rozinka when he had first seen Jara, so young and untried, brimming with carefree youth and laughter. He remembered how he had teased her with the suggestion of a dozen sons for the Jelinek Eleven. He thought of her warmth and her kindness, her skill with the children, her devotion to them and to him. He thought of the loyalty she inspired in those who served them, the admiration her hospitality sparked in their friends. Somehow, his mouth managed to turn up into the semblance of a smile.

"Boys, I am going off with these two officers. I'll return home before long. Meanwhile, take care of your mother and Maria and your new baby brother."

As he leaned down to kiss each of them, he was aware of the smell of the youngsters, the sweet healthy smell of childhood mingling with the aroma of the medicines Anna was using to treat their autumn colds. The boys stared at him, wide-eyed, dimly aware of a dark threat that their young beings felt without completely comprehending. Frank broke first. His eyes reflecting the threat of terror, he threw down his book, flung himself across the pillow and buried his sobs. He was eleven. He was born six months after Hitler came to power in Germany; he knew by osmosis the marrow-chilling terrors of the Nazi regime. He knew the danger to his parent. Fathers of his friends had been snatched away and nothing was ever heard of them again and their sons wandered around, blank-eyed and stunned and silent.

Otto, who was only five, had no inkling of his father's precarious position. Naturally, he loved Father, although he already showed signs of fighting parental authority. But it was really an inopportune moment for Father to appear—just as the story was about to reach its climax. Even before the door to the boys' room closed, Father heard Otto's voice giving Frank an order. "Read on, Frank."

It was different for Richard, who lay rigid on the third bed. Richard was seven and a half years old, already endowed with the soul of a poet; he was emotionally sensitive to the drama Father was determined to underplay. Richard mastered his feelings—up to a point. But as the Gestapo men were leading Father out of the room, down the stairs, through the corridor into the open, Richard leaped out of bed, raced after them, pulling at their coats, crying wildly, "Leave my father alone, you dirty Gestapo pigs! Let him go—or I'll kill you!" The men shoved him away roughly and he fell to the snowy ground.

In the Prague headquarters of the Gestapo, Nazi secret service commissars hauled Father from his cell every day for questioning. They wanted badly to pin something on him; over and over again, they accused him of organizing in his home underground meetings against the German-run government. Then, one evening, as he was once more taken out of his dirty, rat-infested cell, the Nazis changed their tactics. This time, all were cordial and polite. Dr. Gruber, Secret Service Chief in Prague, was in fact most affable.

"What could I offer you to eat, Mr. Jelinek?" he asked amiably. "A little chicken, perhaps, or some ham? You have only to say." Since the Gestapo half starved its prisoners, even those who might be useful to them later, this mention of good food puzzled Father. What were they up to?

Father calmly indicated that his choice was chicken. Dr. Gruber barked an order into his office phone, and soon an attractive young woman arrived with a well prepared meal. It was characteristic of the Nazis to use pretty girls as bait. The portion of chicken, Father recalls, in the way details stay in one's mind in times of crisis, was adequate rather than generous. Instead of offering a second helping, the police chief, who had calmly waited until his prisoner finished what was on the plate, gave him a cigarette.

The prisoner lit up. Dr. Gruber, smiling as he spoke, asked, "How would you like to be released tomorrow morning?"

Father played the game dead-pan, according to the rules. Instead of retorting angrily, "What a tomfool question! Of course, I'd like to get out of here tomorrow morning," he said quietly, "I would like to, very much." The cordiality was obviously false. He knew that it was a trap; he was being led into something very unpleasant.

But the political drama was not yet played out. "Very well, Mr. Jelinek. Tomorrow you can be back at home with your family and the baby you haven't seen yet. You need only to sign this paper."

Feeling that he might as well go along with a procedure he knew to be a farce, Father began to read the paper handed to him. It was a false and fatal confession.

"I admit holding political meetings in my home with the people named below taking part in them, in an attempt to overthrow the German Government."

Then followed a list of prominent Prague citizens. Just that: two lines of indictment and confession. But Father knew that once he signed the paper, not only he but also all the men whose names were on the list would be promptly arrested and executed. His anger flared, despite the risk of adding to his peril.

"Sorry," he said, "I refuse to sign what is not true."

Dr. Gruber took out his gold watch and placed it on the desk before Father. "I give you five minutes to sign this statement," he said.

Father refused. How could he obey? He felt too bitter to be afraid. But the ice was perilously thin.

Promptly to the moment—good timekeeping was ever a German

characteristic—Gruber returned. The paper still blank of signature. Curtly, he summoned two guards.

"Boys," he said to the SS men, of the Gestapo's death-dealing branch, "we shall show Mr. Jelinek how to bowl, Russian style."

The guards smiled.

"Sir," Gruber turned to Father, bitingly, sardonically polite, "Have you ever played a game of Russian bowling?"

"I have not," replied Father, trying to master his growing sense of rage and frustration.

"Then I shall explain it to you on our way to the bowling alley," said the Chief.

In the elevator, Dr. Gruber did indeed explain the game. He described that his men hung a rope in the middle of a large room, so that its end dangled about a foot off the ground. A bowling ball was then attached to the free-swinging rope end. Pins are also in the center of the room. The game was played by swinging the ball from one side, letting it go and trying to knock down as many pins as possible on the first swing. All harmless and amusing, at least in the original Russian version. That is, before the Gestapo changed the rules.

Stepping from the elevator, jailer and prisoner emerged into a large gloomy room. Not one but five heavy ropes hung from the ceiling. There were no pins in the center of the playing area. Instead, tied in an up-side-down position, four men hung from the ceiling, held in agony, by their ankles. On the floor was a pool of drying blood. One rope dangled empty, awaiting another participant to complete the grisly five-a-side.

"Franz!" thundered Gruber. His shout echoed through the dismal abattoir. Franz stepped in from a side door set in the wall. He made the door shrink to a small escape hole, Father thought grimly. For Franz was all of six feet six inches, with neck and shoulders massive as a bull's.

"Here, sir," he said, a respectful giant standing stiffly at attention.

"You will show our new friend how well you bowl." Gruber looked angrily at Father. Then a sardonic smile flitted across his pinched face.

Franz strode over to the men hanging by the ropes. He pushed one human bowling ball out into the opposite corner, as far as the rope would go. Then with a turn of speed surprising in a clumsy giant, he dashed in turn to the other tied-up men, hauling each of them as far apart as the length of rope would allow. On the return swing the four Czech heads, inevitably collided.

As their heads crashed against each other in a bloody mess, the helpless prisoners screamed in agony. Feeling sick, Father turned his head away to avoid seeing what he could not fail to hear. Gruber was watching him, rather than the ghastly game. Perhaps even his sadistic emotions were already sated. Nevertheless, with another guard standing by, ready to help, he jerked father's head around so that it was in line with the field of play. "You'll never learn how to play this bowling game unless you watch carefully," he said with a rough sarcasm.

"Franz," he roared again, "Show this fellow once more how it goes."

Several more "frames," and Gruber signalled the play to stop. The players, silent now, had lapsed into bloody but merciful unconsciousness. Gruber motioned Father to follow him and stalked to the room where Father had been given the ultimatum.

Out came the gold watch again. "You have five minutes to sign," Gruber said. He tried to push the pen into Father's hand. "You sign, or"—as if the prospective new member of the Gestapo torture play team needed a reminder—"this time you will be the fifth pin."

The fifth pin. Sick with fear and terror of the horrifying sight he had just been made to witness, Father still refused to put his name to the incriminating document.

Gruber waited.

The two men glowered at one another in a silence of hatred and frustration. Before the five minutes had ticked to its end, Gruber evidently realized he was the loser. In a wild rage, he jumped up, banged on the table, and ordered father frog-marched back to his cell. Back to the world of solitary confinement.

Nobody will ever know why—and I have long ceased to pester my father on the point—Gruber gave up after that encounter. In his cell, Father remained apprehensive, giving way to an onrush of momentary fear, even panic, whenever heavy feet crunched up to his cell door. Fully half of the men the Gestapo took inside their bowling alley emerged as corpses. But for Father, after that excruciating day, the Gestapo questioning was routine, almost formal. No open trial, of course, but no real grilling either.

Perhaps the Gestapo found another way of getting at the men whose names were on the list of supposed conspirators. Father remained in close confinement and in great peril. But even if he had been sent back home, he would have still had cause to fear, as thousands in Prague had cause to fear, the heavy tread outside the door, the knock that announced the arrival of the security guards of the Nazi Reich.

The difference was that here in prison, day and night, Father was entirely in the sight and power of his SS warders. He was slight in build at the start of his imprisonment, but by its end, he had lost thirty pounds.

How do you measure days in solitary confinement? Father thinks he served at least a month. To Mother and the children on the outside, it seemed even longer.

After being only with himself for a month, Father was transferred to a cell already occupied by two other Czech political prisoners. The place was small, gloomy and damp. For a bed, each man had a wood plank, six feet long and one wide. A hole in the middle of the concrete floor served for sanitary needs and was seldom cleaned. The prisoners received a ration twice daily of bread and water.

At first, solitary confinement was an excruciating ordeal for Father. He is a warm, gregarious man, an extrovert who is happiest among his family and friends. To deprive him of all means of communication was a sadistic punishment. Yet in a short while, Father discovered he was not alone. If he were unable to communicate with the world, God proved to be a good listener. Father had never before understood why monks, for instance, should make a retreat. But now, it came to him that enforced silence might have a therapeutic effect. It gave you time for looking inward, for evaluating the circumstances of life, for seeking a clue to the puzzling web of fate.

The Czechs as a nation are deeply religious, and Father had always accepted religion as a part of his nature. But in those outwardly empty and silent days, it became a vital living force, more nourishing than the bread and water handed to him by his grudging captors.

Father never made a production of it. But later, to the family, it was evident that his faith had deepened under those grim circumstances, and that its strength made it possible for him to face what lay ahead. God's plans may seem unpredictable to the human who is momentarily a victim, but Father's firm belief in God's love made it possible in the end for him and his family to survive.

Now that the rule of silence was no longer enforced, Father made friends with his cellmates. They talked in spurts of their homes and families, although the subject grew painful after a few minutes.

Then they would switch to verbal memories of the old days in Prague. The old free days that now seemed incredible. Freedom to walk through the city parks. Freedom to join a group of friends sitting over coffee in the Nabrezi Slavia cafes. They remembered how they had strolled along the banks of the Moldau River, tossing crumbs to the birds that wheeled under the arched bridges. They remembered feats of feathered seamanship, with birds perched on tiny ice floes as the spring thaw put the river in spate.

They agreed it was good to dwell in company, even though the dwelling place was a damp dungeon. They saved crusts from their meager rations and out of bits of bread, they fashioned rough chessmen, pawns, castles and knights. Using their fingernails, they carved out of the cell floor a board of squares and engaged in games of chess, taking their time over each move, since it was thus that free men played.

Time passed. Slowly. But it passed.

For Mother, it was a time of chilling terror. During Father's absence, she had to answer the children's questions as best she could and maintain a composure that would lull their fears. In the crisis, she proved herself capable of keeping a clear head, just as Father had anticipated.

She spent a great deal of time with the children, and it was during this period that she told the older ones about her ancestor, the Hussite general Jan Zizka. Perhaps the idea was to inculcate courage within them; perhaps it was to compound her own faith.

Frank and Richard have since told me the stories that she used to relate to them, mainly about her ancestor, the Hussite general, Jan Zizka.

No contemporary conqueror can ever diminish the reputation of Zizka. He is firmly entrenched as one of the great Czech heroes. His was an obstinate, unflagging drive for freedom. And the Zizka courage and fortitude descended not only from father to son, but father to daughter. He was called One-Eyed Jan, for he had lost an eye in battle under the ruler Wenceslaus—not the Wenceslaus of Christmas carol fame, but another warrior, who fought for Prague nearly five-hundred years later. In a subsequent battle, Zizka lost the sight of his good eye. Completely blinded and in agony, he nevertheless kept his command, displaying a fantastic hold on men's allegiance and a genius for rallying his soldiers through hopeless sieges.

It was a whim of fate that he died in a battlefield, not of cannon shot or rapier thrust but of a plague virus.

Legends suggest he was determined to fight on even after death. As he lay dying, he ordered that once rigor mortis set in, his body was to be skinned, and from the skin a drum was to be fashioned— a drum to summon his warriors to wherever the tide of battle might be turning against them.

His passing didn't weaken the Bohemian armies, for while he was sightless he had taught his lieutenants and aides de camp— according to Czech historians—"to notice the advantage afforded by the disposition of the ground, or by his own experience in the distribution of his forces." However, after his death, political schism showed itself among his followers. Some called themselves "The Orphans" in tribute to the dead leader. Others, who had conspired against Zizka, saw in the schism a chance for negotiating with their foreign enemies. Appeasement is not a new trait in human nature. It was as rampant in the fifteenth century as today. At that time, German nobles and princes began to take up arms against the "Bohemian heretics." The uprising was in the name of religion, as it served primarily as a cloak for territorial greed. The medieval version of the German "drive to the east," was on. And even then, the Czech people were standing in its way.

Zizka's cause suffered a setback. The flowering of Czech nation-

alism was checked for centuries. The broad stream of political
and religious reform was hindered. However, if Zizka's sightless
eyes can no longer survey the scene of battle, his fierce, independent spirit lives on in his descendants—millions of them. His
courage is his memorial.

We Jelineks were never allowed to forget it.

Mother now assumed the role of provider and bread-winner.
Besides caring for us and the servants, she found it necessary to
give much thought to the future of the family business.

The Jelinek cork plant was being run by Germans for the
benefit of German armament and German industry. Mother decided to pave the way for its return to the family. In order to
execute the plan, it was essential for her to discover who among
the officials and administrators was open to bribe. Since it was
evident to those Nazis with inside information that the great
dream of a thousand year Reich was coming to an abrupt and
rude end, they were more susceptible to offers of cash.

Mother used most of her gold resources not for the business but
to ransom Father from prison. It began to look as though her
bargaining efforts would work. After the money was delivered, an
unknown voice over the telephone told her, "He will be out before
Christmas."

Mother brightened; she alerted the children. Suddenly, the
future lost its threat. It would be a poor Christmas as far as
material goodies were concerned, but the family would be together, and that was the most precious gift Mother could hope for.

Christmas night arrived. Mother could scarcely contain her
excitement. But the night dragged on, and there was no sign of
Father, and finally, her indomitable spirits admitted defeat. He
wasn't coming; his captors had reneged. It was probable that the
negotiations had been discovered and might even put his life once
more in peril.

Nevertheless, Mother dogged the man who had taken her money
in a solemn exchange for Father's freedom.

His excuses sounded reasonable. Only one more signature was
necessary, he assured her, to complete the formalities for Father's
release. The signature was forthcoming and on his honor, the man
promised, Father would be home a Friday night after the New
Year.

Henry Jelinek, Sr. (*center*) in uniform as a second lieutenant in the Czechoslovakian cavalry (1919).

Henry and Jarmilla Jelinek courting by the Moldau river (1929).

Maria and Henry, Jr. in Canada (1949).

Maria and Otto dressed for church in Prague (1946).

Maria and Otto in Switzerland (1948).

Henry Jelinek, Sr. and his oldest son Frank on the Czechoslovak-German border (1938).

The Jelineks in Switzerland after the escape (1948). *Bottom:* Otto, Maria, Henry, Jr., Mrs. Jelinek, Richard. *Top:* Henry, Sr. and Frank.

Maria and Otto (1958).

Maria and Otto (1947).

Mother was an optimist because she needed to be. "Let us prepare for Father," she said gaily. The children, dressed in fresh clothes, sat waiting, eager and wonderfully well behaved.

It was a long wait. Mother finally put me to bed. Then Maria, still tiny, began to droop and then fell asleep. Finally Otto's eyes closed. And Richard's. Frank was the last to give in. But eventually he yielded to Mother's entreaties and trotted off to bed, on the condition that as the man of the family—he was then eleven—he was to be awakened the minute Father arrived.

Mother was left alone, bereft and stunned. She sat quietly, in the shabby finery of her pre-war wardrobe. She did not cry but the tears were swelling in her heart.

Street noises ceased as the hour of curfew arrived. She knew then that it would not be. Her husband would not return that night, nor perhaps any other night. The house was still as death. Her children were over-tired with the strain of waiting. They slept soundly. The hours dragged into dawn. There was not even the sound of Gestapo boots in the street.

Father's ordeal was not yet over. It lasted for more than three months.

What finally brought about his release was neither the bribe nor the softening of the Nazi heart. It was the simple fact that the Allies were closing in on the Nazis from east and west. The Germans sensed the war was terminating, and they were doomed to defeat. Concerned with self-preservation, they began to ease the pressure on the Czech citizens. In the days of that last cold winter of war in Europe, Czechs said openly to each other, "It won't be long now." They even discarded the habit of the furtive glance over the shoulders to make sure no German in uniform was in sight.

The small valiant Czech underground came out in the open. With innocent good will, the Resistance linked up with the advancing Red Army, whose presence was soon to open another bitter chapter in Czech history. But for the moment, the sky above the golden spires of Prague was bright with the hopes of a people on the eve of a second liberation.

The ice, in those days of high expectations, was once again firm under the feet of the Jelineks.

chapter four

THE WARTIME HISTORY OF CZECHOSLOVAKIA HAD its scroll of fame and infamy. The association of ill repute belongs to one man, Reinhard Heydrich, Protector of Bohemia and Moravia. Heidrich, the Hangman; Heidrich, the Butcher.

The fame belongs to Lidice.

Lidice was the heroic little town whose houses and roads were wiped off the map one day, its men slaughtered, because it had aided the Czech patriots who had assassinated Heydrich.

A man needs the cold dispassionate approach of a historian to write calmly about Heydrich. But this is an impossible role for a Czech. Even after twenty-three years, the horror is still with us.

Reinhard Heydrich was the Number Two man in the Nazi hierarchy to Heinrich Himmler, head of the secret State Police. Heydrich was sent to Prague by Hitler as a successor to the first Protector of Bohemia and Moravia, these being the only two provinces left to Czechoslovakia after the German grab in 1939. Heydrich followed Baron von Neurath who was called "Gentleman" Neurath for reasons we have never divined. Perhaps there was a suggestion of gentleness in the Baron that ill suited Hitler's thirst for ruthlessness and brutality. Anyway, Heydrich was evidently Hitler's personal choice for the job. Once Heydrich arrived on the scene, it was clear that Hacha, the tame Czech republican

44

president, had no say at all. From the day Heydrich became by force the resident of Hradcany castle, he was determined to bring the Czech citizens to bloody heel.

Meanwhile, in England, Czech patriots were plotting the death of Heydrich. They sent to Prague secret orders for the assassination, indicating how Czech citizens within the Nazi fort could be of help.

In the dark silence of a December night in 1941, a team of men sworn to political murder swung down to the soil of their Czech homeland; they were harnessed in parachutes that had opened at 2,000 feet. They went into hiding with the assistance of the Underground. Moving secretly about the country, they recruited other brave men. It was May 27, 1942, when they were finally prepared, with bullets and bomb, to put an end to the assassin of the Czech nation.

They struck early that morning, as Heydrich's car passed through a Prague suburb.

They hit their target.

According to the first official announcement from Berlin, Heydrich died seven days later. In those seven days, Nazi rage boiled over in a lava of fury that scorched every Czech citizen.

Directly after the assassination, the police ordered a curfew, the registration of every Prague citizen before midnight of the following day, and a warning of death by firing squad of entire families, if one member sheltered the assassins.

These orders were followed by mass arrests and executions.

"Helping fugitives to evade the authorities," was a capital crime.

"Approving the assassination," was another fatal phrase used by the Germans to excuse their wholesale slaughter of those innocent Czech citizens who actually got their knowledge of the assassination from the official radio bulletins. Nazi judges and firing squads read men's minds to suit their ends. Prisoners in Prague jails, who had been shut away for earlier political offenses long before Heydrich's death, were pulled from their cells and condemned for "approving the assassination."

But the bloody interrogations brought the Germans no trace of the heroic Czech fighters who had removed The Butcher. Nor even of the men and women of the Resistance who had first organized the daring scheme.

The Nazis offered rewards mounting into improbable sums. In the vicinity of Prague alone, well over a million citizens were hauled up for interrogation. According to official Nazi documents, about 1,293 Czechs were killed in this roundup. But according to the Czechs, this number falls far short of the total slaughtered in the Nazis' mad lust for vengeance. The records are incomplete. If each death were certified, the mind would fail to comprehend the enormity of that orgy of annihilation. One figure, published with the official authority of Czech statisticans to support it, indicates that throughout the country 4,715,501 people were questioned in the search for Heydrich's slayers.

As the grillings and shootings mounted, the spotlight focused on Lidice, a township nearing the mining center of Kladno, about twenty miles from Prague. The official Protectorate news agency, which was under the strictest Nazi control, announced that proof beyond doubt indicated that the inhabitants of Lidice had "helped and supported the circle of those responsible" for the assassination of Heydrich. This proof has been obtained, the Agency announced blandly, "without the help of the citizens of this place."

Once it had been established that Lidice had indeed harbored the Resistance group helping the assassins, had provided secret radio links with the outside world, had hidden arms and ammunition, the Nazis ruled that Lidice did not deserve to live.

As murderers, the Nazis were perfectionists. Accordingly, 176 male inhabitants, between the ages of 14 and 76, were slaughtered in the peaceful garden of a Lidice farm. Then the women were transported to concentration camps. The children were shipped off to "appropriate" institutions. Not a living soul remained. But that was not enough to appease the Nazi appetite for vengeance. So the village was burnt to the ground. Bulldozers were dispatched to erase the ruins. Even the Lidice brook was diverted from its tranquil bed.

That the United States was the first country to insure the survival of the name of Lidice by renaming American towns in honor of the martyred community, was of some consolation to the grief stricken Czechs. But as the savage act passed into history, the world gradually forgot it.

Not so with the Czechs. And specifically, not our family. For in that year of 1942, when the hunt was at its inhuman height, there was a cruel impact on our family.

It happened at 2:30 of a summer's morning, when the household was deep in troubled sleep. A woman servant was awakened first by the banging on the heavy front door.

"Aufmachen!" shouted the visitors. "Open up!"

The Nazis at the door did not wait to be ushered in. They used their rifle butts to smash in the door. Before the maid could get down to them, they were tramping through the house, six pairs of heavy murderous boots, six pairs of deadly blank eyes, in search of the killers of Heydrich.

They stormed through the house in a whirlwind of destruction. They jabbed their bayonets into the sofas, they slashed paintings, they stabbed at the walls in hope of locating an entrance to a secret hiding place.

Awakened by the tumult, Father dashed downstairs. The havoc left him speechless. The bullies, working in the dining room, had slashed the walls draped in priceless silk fabrics to shreds.

They pushed Father aside and roared up the stairs and into our parents' bedroom. Mother was sitting up in bed, trembling with fright. For she knew that any man who was found still to possess his weapons (even antique ones), books written by persecuted authors and his Czechoslovakian army uniform was in danger of being shot. The invaders slashed everything in the room, including her mattress. Finally, they stomped out, leaving the brand of their destruction on the house.

"The search for the guilty ones goes on," the official radio announced. "Unless the murderers are found within three days every tenth man in the Protectorate will be shot."

The city was paralyzed; terror froze the heart and limbs. Friends dared not to communicate with one another. Visiting was a dangerous enterprise, even by day. One night, Peter Novak, a family friend, arrived surreptitiously for dinner. He was staying in Prague during the reign of terror; his abode was on the outskirts of Lidice and nothing had been heard of his wife and three children since the sack of the village. He sat at the table like a crucified man. Only his voice was alive. He told us of a friend who had been savagely beaten to death by the Gestapo men.

"They were ransacking his house in search of Heydrich's assassins and they found his old Czech uniform hanging in a closet," Peter said.

"My uniform, my revolver and hundreds of books are hidden under old rubbish in the cellar," Father said, "but I was sick with anxiety when those bullies came into our house. I was terrified they would find it."

Not long afterwards, the Gestapo got a tip that the killers of Heydrich were hidden in the crypt of a church. The Nazis brought up a whole army to dislodge them. At bayonet point, they forced the Prague Fire Brigade into action. Hoses flooded the crypt; guns blazed.

But the heroic Czechs did not yield to fire or water.

They died by their own hands.

The war years gave the Jelineks quite a legacy to carry with them to the new country.

And our parents never allowed us to forget it.

Among the four Jelinek sons, Otto lays claim to fame for a number of reasons, not all of them flattering. But it is true that he was, at the age of five, eye witness to the battle in Prague that dispelled most of the German army. He was in Father's office, and during the battle in the streets, when the Germans were routed, Father was a participant, blazing away with enormous zest from behind a window in his office.

Now that the smell of victory was in the air and Czech hearts were warmed with the knowledge that the Wehrmacht was in retreat on both fronts, Father and Otto always walked from our home each Saturday morning into the city.

It is worth recording why Otto, although the third of the Jelinek sons, was already avidly absorbed in the strategy of battle. Response to challenge was his birthright.

Otto was from babyhood the family Character, full of charm and pranks, an extraordinary combination of the Zizka and Jelinek genes. In the rambling Prague house, the children's playroom was on the third floor. Here most of the toys were assembled. Otto owned a rocking horse, a fierce gallant steed with a magnificent mane. Otto, the racehorse owner, was the envy of his friends, but

Otto was not one to be satisfied with conditions as they were. There was clearly a difference between his steed and the horses working on the farms. What was missing in his toy? he demanded. Why didn't it respond to verbal orders? Since no one could explain to his satisfaction, Otto did an exploratory on his horse's head. With an axe.

Then finding mayhem to his liking, he continued the carnage. Since the family doctor had encouraged our parents to exercise our arms and legs as infants, Otto had superb muscular coordination. He put his throwing arm enthusiastically to the task. He wasn't discovered until he had emptied the playroom of all furniture and toys it was possible to shove through the window.

When Otto was about six, he used to swear a great deal. His grandmother Zizka explained that swearing made the angels very sad and the devils supremely happy. And when the angels were upset, it meant Santa Claus wouldn't be bringing him any more presents.

When Grandmother put Otto to bed one evening, she asked earnestly, "Otto, did you swear today?"

"I did not," Otto said solemnly.

"That is good," Grandmother replied, "that will make the angels happy."

"That may be so," he replied, "but the devils will be goddamn mad as hell."

Otto's early life seemed to consist of a series of pranks and minor crises that kept the family in a state of nerves. During this period, Mother reprimanded him for having hit Maria over the head with a tennis racket. Her scolding shattered Otto. He pointed out with rare Otto-logic, "But, Mommy, don't you appreciate my strength? I actually broke the racket over her head."

Shortly after he learned to skate, Otto discovered the delightful evils of tobacco. He was then no more than six, and naturally anything that was forbidden assumed a terrific allure for him. He collected butts on the street and out of Father's ashtrays. He could break these up in a box, mix the tobacco and expertly roll a cigarette. He was observed several times hiding behind a tree and enjoying a smoke. When he was discovered smoking at school, the teacher said, "Otto, why just cigarettes? Try this."

Otto accepted the cigar politely and lit it.

"You must inhale," the teacher insisted.

Some time later, a friend of the family jokingly offered him a cigarette. Otto declined.

"Thank you very much, sir," he said seriously, "but I gave up smoking several months ago."

Knowing a little about Otto's character makes it simpler even for the rest of us Jelineks to understand why he was the one who accompanied Father wherever there was an indication of a street melee.

The German retreat from Prague was in full swing. Nevertheless, a Nazi commander, who later refused to acknowledge even the Germans' order for unconditional surrender, was determined to stage a battle in the center of the city. So the Czech Resistance Fighters, ably assisted by men like Father (with Otto on the office sidelines and not nearly as safe from injury as Father hoped), fought valiantly.

The American Army was only seven miles outside the city and wheeling into a position from which they were never allowed to advance. For the Russians, with a single brutish purpose which was misinterpreted by the Allies, were completing their encirclement of Prague.

Our beautiful old city went through the whole German occupation and the war without suffering much material damage to the buildings. But that final battle in the center of town, which Otto witnessed, resulted in the wrecking of the Town Hall and the famous fifteenth century clock on its façade.

In 1952, during the third year of our family's new life in Canada, Otto, though still struggling with the intricacies of the English language, managed to record his unique war experience in an article. It was called "The Ruins of a Town Hall" and was printed in his school's yearbook:

There was once a boy who was born at the beginning of World War II. Every Saturday, the boy's father used to take him downtown to his office. Nearby was the Town Hall with a magnificent clock which, every hour, played lovely music while different figures of saints and gnomes moved about. The boy looked forward to this scene every week.

On such a lovely spring day, the first Saturday of May, 1945, he and his father again watched the clock with great interest. Then, as usual, they went to the office.

Suddenly, the boy saw that civilians were fighting with soldiers, the same soldiers that had occupied their country throughout the entire war. He saw the people tear the uniforms off the soldiers and disarm them and even shoot some of the enemy. In other words, a revolution had started.

After a while, soldiers came driving their tanks right into the people. Aeroplanes flew over the city, throwing bombs at random. The boy was hidden behind a window which suddenly shattered. The glass flew all over the office. The boy ran to hide behind his father who was kneeling at another window, shooting. This incident continued for three days and nights without letup. Neither the boy nor his father left the office, nor did they eat or sleep properly.

When everything was over and the soldiers had to leave town, the boy and his father left for their home. Naturally, they stopped at the Town Hall to look at the clock with its saints and gnomes. How surprised they were not to see the Town Hall nor the lovely clock. What they saw was the ruins of the place they had loved.

Both stood watching the ruins and like others, silently cried.

> This story is no imagination.
> It's a true history of a poor nation.
> It happened in Czechoslovakia's capital city,
> When the Germans were driven out without pity;
> For the broken clock, I felt very sorry.
> So you can recognize the boy in the story.

Otto would probably challenge me to a duel—with fists—if he knew I called him a sentimentalist. But he is. Even as a child, he saw with his heart.

The family had endured, along with all of Prague, three days of the most dreadful confusion and terror.

Our house was situated on the Hradcany Hill and was therefore a natural defense site for the Germans, who still held captive that section of the city. The soldiers encamped in our garden were the S.S. troops, composed mainly of Sudeten Germans, who were a particular source of danger to the citizens of Prague, since they understood the Czech language. They dug foxholes in the lower slope of the garden and placed machine guns at vantage points, so the lovely flower beds became a military encampment.

Father and Otto were still trapped in the old part of town, while Mother, the other children and the servants, found partial safety in our home. Fortunately, the house was built seven hundred years previously, so the massive walls of ancient stone and the deep cellars afforded a natural sanctuary for the family. Anna and the other members of the staff had lugged mattresses and food into the wine cellar, which was our air raid shelter during the entire war. Here all of us lived for those three memorable days, except for such intervals as Mother felt it necessary to replenish food or to make an attempt to communicate with Father.

Naturally, she was desperately anxious for Father and Otto during that three day siege. She knew that Father's office was extremely vulnerable to the bombings of the Germans and the advance of the Russians and the Czech Resistance fighters. Whenever he found it possible, Father telephoned from his office to the house. There was a telephone in the kitchen, which was nearest to the cellar, and it was this one Mother always answered.

During this hectic time, when the world was filled with the thunder of bombardments and the chatter of machine guns, the Germans in our garden would come up to the kitchen windows and demand water or other necessities. One of them happened to overhear Mother talking on the telephone that second day to Father. Evidently this was a Sudeten German for he said roughly, "Your husband is a spy! If you telephone him once more and report to him what is going on here, I will shoot you!"

It was for Mother a double crisis. She gathered from Father's message that the Russians were advancing. Yet here she was, trapped in the heart of a German encampment. Aware of the reputed sadism of the S.S. troopers, she couldn't believe they would withdraw, leaving her and the children and the staff safe. Their actions had always been associated in her mind with the most vicious carnage, like Lidice. So she waited in agony, and all the while, it was her duty to assuage the fears of the servants, to calm the children and to nourish the child at her breast.

That third day, she could bear imprisonment no longer. In the promise of dusk, she stepped out of the dark cellar into the gardens. The blend of firs and bullets assailed her nostrils. The bodies of the Storm troopers seemed to merge with the shrubbery.

How long can we hold out, how long will we be safe here? She asked herself. When the city is free at last, will we be here to celebrate?

During the debacle, there was much confusion overhead. Nobody knew whether the strafing planes were English, American, Russian—or German. During a sudden fresh outburst of fire, the Storm troopers dived into their foxholes. Mother was left standing, unprotected, in the shadow of the house. But one German officer approached her, revolver in hand. She tensed in fear. He pulled her into the house. In silence, they watched and listened. Now the sound of the approaching Russians grew louder.

"They are perhaps five minutes away," he said in German, "It is all over."

Mother was trembling.

"Tomorrow—" It was almost as though he were talking to himself, "Your flag will be flying in the Square. You will be celebrating—with cakes and wine and song. Victory is so sweet—"

He reached into his breast pocket, took out a small leather case and handed it to Mother. She opened it and in the fading light, she made out the pictures of a woman and three small girls, flaxen haired and smiling.

"Mine," he said. "They died in the bombing. For me, there is nothing left. Defeat of my country, death of my family—" He held up the revolver. "The last bullet—it is for me."

The sense of confusion remained during the rest of the third day. Father and Otto returned safely and were greeted with exclamations of joy and emotional embraces. The talk was general, with no one really listening but trying to give his own version of the military bedlam.

The Germans who had made an impromptu fort of our gardens sneaked away in the dusk. However, two of them stayed behind; they were tough obstinate Storm Troopers who evidently figured that their devotion to the Fuhrer demanded the last ounce of their resistance. As a result, they manned their machine gun, at the left section of the garden, with a vicious enthusiasm that spattered bullets into the courtyard facing the gardens and chipped the outside walls of the library wing of the house.

This barrage, coming at erratic intervals, was naturally a source of danger to the family, particularly the children who, having been so long confined, were now determined to get outdoors to play. To have endured so much and yet to remain in danger when the Russians were already in possession of the city aroused Father to action. He telephoned the Military Headquarters and asked for assistance.

Shortly, there was a pounding on the heavy wood door; the gardener opened up and a Russian sergeant marched in, followed by a half dozen of his men. The gardener gesticulated toward the trouble spot and they continued through the courtyard, when Father, spying them, shouted a warning through the library window.

"Careful, you're in the line of fire! Go no farther—or you'll be killed—"

The sergeant turned to Father. He said curtly, "It doesn't matter. If we are killed, there are millions of others . . ."

He waved his men to proceed. Then there was a burst of machine gun fire. The sergeant fell, his head nearly cut in half by bullets. The soldier directly behind him toppled over, horribly wounded. The third man paused and signalled his men to retreat to the gate.

Shortly, a wave of Russians appeared, and after a few minutes, fire from the machine gun nest at the foot of the garden was heard no more.

The troubles of the siege, particularly the third day, were not yet over. The Russian occupation brought new hazards for the Jelineks. This time, however, the danger came from another source.

Somebody once said, "Save me from my friends and I'll take care of my enemies." We could have switched that around to, "Save us from our relatives . . ."

Now, do not misunderstand. We Jelineks were blessed with good friends and loyal relatives. But a few of our family not only tried Father's patience but actually endangered our lives.

One of these was Edward Vopicka. He was distantly related to us, and our parents were indulgent with him, as one is indulgent with a difficult child. But after the war, he was more destructive to our family than any malicious child ever could be.

My father has always been fond of *The Good Soldier Schweik,* the legendary bumbling fictional hero who has two left feet. Schweik's secret weapon was his naivete. Schweik bluffed his way out of the most difficult situations.

Schweik and our Vopicka both had an uncanny instinct for survival. Whereas farmyard aromas saturated Schweik's clothes, Vopicka was a clean smelling city-bred upstart, who existed by his wits.

Poor Schweik was an addled, inoffensive, tubby character, trusting the world. Vopicka, tall and voracious, hair slicked down, nose sharp as an ant-eater's, was forever seeking out his next victim.

There are many Schweiks in the Communist-dominated lands and even more Vopickas.

Before Czechoslovakia was endowed with a place on the map of the world, Vopicka managed to live adequately under the Austrian-Hungarian rule. As a matter of fact, no Emperor could wish for a more loyal follower. Previous to the German invasion of the new republic of Czechoslovakia, he was a righteous citizen and a voluble democrat. However, once the Wehrmacht began its formidable goosestepping through the cobbled streets of Prague, Vopicka found himself a comfortable new political philosophy. "Our neighbors, the Germans, are pretty fine fellows," he announced solemnly. That they were Nazis who were bent on destroying our valiant little country didn't matter to him. He had blinders to keep him from seeing what was not useful to his future. Finally, when the Russians and the Resistance made a clean sweep of the Germans, he agreed that this was a move not only of expedience but of political virtue. Vopicka embraced Communism like the body of a ravishing woman.

And if Father had not had enough problems that wild third day, there was still the shattering encounter with Vopicka. Vopicka presented quite a picture. He swaggered into Father's library, unsteady on his feet not only with a conqueror's liquor but with the guns and cartridge belts that weighed him down. He pulled a gun out of his pocket and announced with a flourish, "You see, it's still smoking. I just killed two Germans with this gun." As if to emphasize his point, he removed a second gun from the other pocket. Trying to focus on Father, to gauge his reaction, Vopicka repeated, "I've just killed two Germans. Now, I've got my eye on you capitalists. Your turn comes next."

In the midst of his threat, the telephone rang. Father answered it, and discovered the caller was a Gestapo agent. This once brutal, sadistic creature was now reduced to a state of terrified hysterics. He was in hiding. He had always tried to do his best for Herr Jelinek—he assured Father—and now, couldn't Herr Jelinek be magnanimous and do something for him, since he had been forced to join the Gestapo, since he had always been against the Gestapo, since he was a member of the Nazi party only to help wreck it.

What a familiar alibi! The Nazi Storm Troopers who had scuttled into hiding were now using this plea to any Czech who might show them ill-deserved pity. Perhaps this little monster was telling the truth. Perhaps the circumstances of the Hitler regime had molded him into the straw soldier, who under Hitler's rule, was able to retaliate for the petty injustices meted out to him by the world. But even if he were himself an innocent victim of political chance, how could Father help him?

And had Vopicka known that a Nazi on the run was contacting Father, it would have been bad for the Jelineks.

Fortunately, Vopicka, playing happily with his guns, took no heed of the telephone call. He was much too absorbed in the spiel he was about to launch.

"Things will be different now," Vopicka proclaimed. "Some of you capitalists could fool the Nazis. But not the Communists. The Communist regime won't allow itself to be taken in."

Vopicka was right, and his utterance was his own epitaph. No man fools the Communists easily. They can be stupid on occasion. But when it comes to ruthlessness and persistence, the Nazis just weren't in their league. Yet Vopicka managed to persuade the Communists that he would be loyal to them. Or perhaps they understood him well, and used him and many other Vopickas for their merciless goals.

That afternoon, our chauffeur had equipped himself to deal with Vopicka.

"What's the idea?" Father asked the chauffeur.

"The idea is to protect you. If necessary, I will shoot it out with him."

This was the climate of Prague in those days of confusion. It was often impossible to tell friend from foe. Gestapo men, now fugitive from the Reds, came to us in the dark of the night, begging to be allowed the sanctuary of our cellars. Most Czechs were naturally bitter. And yet, in all of our elders, the streak of humanity was strong. Later, we heard Father ask "Who can judge the reaction of a man under pressure; who understands the breaking point unless he himself has been subjected to torture? Who has insight into the spiritual and emotional tolerance level of a human being?"

Father had to deal with many versions of Vopicka during the Nazi occupation and later during the rule of the Communists. It is to Father's credit that no matter how dangerous the situation was, he never knuckled down to the tyrants. When so many of his friends became political weathervanes, Father learned that false masters are invariably transformed into cowering slaves. The wheel of political expediency becomes the rack of the Inquisition.

Father is sometimes overwhelming in his standards for us. But it's awfully hard to argue with a man who showed such fortitude and courage in the face of terror.

chapter five

THE GERMANS HAD FINALLY DEPARTED, AGAINST
their will, escorted by the weapons of the Resistance. The Russian
troops, however, remained with us. Since there were not enough
Army barracks to accommodate them, the hordes were quartered
in schools, libraries, museums and every private house with even
a minimum of extra space.

We Jelineks were therefore unwilling hosts to a Red Army
colonel and his orderly. The colonel was from a division that had
been famous in front-line battle, consisting of the cream of the
Russian military might. They were superior on the battlefield but
the truth was that they weren't housebroken.

We gave our Russians a room each, complete with bed and
separate bathroom. The orderly, however, slept on the floor, not
because he objected to eiderdown but due to the orders of his
superior. The colonel was unbelievably arrogant to his servant.
The poor fellow was the constant object of beatings, which he
endured with stoic silence. Naturally, this compounded the strains
of having such uncouth house-guests.

The morning after the Russians spent their first night with us,
Father was in his study, working on business papers, when the
maid rushed in, greatly distressed.

"Sir, upstairs—the paper basket is—I think they used the basket
instead of the bathroom—" she exclaimed, indignant and embarrassed.

When the officer returned in the evening, Father asked him for an explanation.

"It is too high for us," was the astonishing reply. "We are used to squatting—as on the battlefield."

As on the battlefield, the Russians were too often trigger happy. They shot my aunt's favorite chuvash dog. They also shot my brother, Frank, squarely between the eyes. Not literally; the target was a portrait of him that hung in our parents' bedroom, above Father's headboard.

The shooting occurred as dawn was breaking. The Russian colonel, rolling home after a night on the town, clearly in search of his vodka breakfast, flung open the door of the room and pulled his gun.

The sound of the door awakened Father. He opened his eyes to find himself staring into the barrel of a pistol. "Now," said the colonel, "I will shoot Frank between the eyes." The shot came before he had time to ask for an explanation. But even in his stupor, the Russian showed himself to be a superior marksman.

Father was unharmed.

Frank's picture hanging above Father's head fell, shattered.

Thus, we learned to accommodate ourselves to the whims of the Russian liberators, and as far as we were concerned, it was no testimonial to pleasant international relations. However, the demands it made upon our patience proved valuable for us in the crucial times still ahead.

What a contradiction the Russians are!

To them, the shooting of a little dog was merely an exercise in marksmanship. They were astonished to discover that the murder of the little creature reduced my aunt to tears. And once their soft Slav hearts were touched, they decided to make amends. Whereupon they tramped all over town looking for a horse to steal. When they finally succeeded, they brought the elderly steed to her, explaining that it should be a consolation, since it was far bigger than the dog she was so distressed about.

In the vicinity of my aunt's country house on the outskirts of Prague, Father owned an estate which was now housing close to three hundred Russians. There were soldiers who, once the big advance had started, were allowed to go to war accompanied by wives and offspring following in wagons and trailers.

One warm spring afternoon, we were gathered in the country house. Father was relaxing in the library when Mother hurried in, her cheeks flushed with embarrassment.

"Come, quickly," she begged.

Father followed her reluctantly into the garden and stopped short. A crowd of Russians, men, women and children, perhaps seventy of them and all nude, were cavorting around the large fish pool. They were having a fine time, running, swimming, splashing each other. One massive woman, built like a wrestler, grabbed a slight man and, lifting him high over her head, sent him flying into the water.

Meanwhile, on the other side of the pool, a man suddenly started shouting. He was holding something heavy in his hand, and at the sound of his voice, the swimmers cleared hurriedly out of the water, after which he tossed the object into the pond.

It was a grenade. The Reds didn't fish with hook and line. They tossed a grenade into the water and then scooped up the dead fish. This was, to us, a frightening indication of the people with whom we were dealing.

We soon saw another side to their behavior. At the country house, Father also had an office. He had to allow a Russian general its use. One day while Father and the general were working in the office, one of the maids came in, weeping.

"Sir," she cried, "just a few moments ago I walked into my room, and as I opened the door I saw a soldier jump out of the window. He ran off with my watch."

Father calmed her hysteria by promising to replace the timepiece with a new one, and she left, placated.

The Russian and the Czech languages are similar, and the general had partly understood what transpired. He approached Father's desk.

"The woman said something about a watch. Tell me about it."

"Oh, it is nothing; do not worry about it, general."

"I insist you tell me, sir," commanded the general.

Reluctantly, Father related the story. The Russian turned around and stalked out. Several minutes later the roll-call trumpet sounded. A young officer marched into Father's room and said the general wished to see him outside.

Father saw two long rows of men standing at attention in front of the building.

"Would you summon the woman whose watch was stolen?" the general asked Father.

The maid was called.

"Now," said the general to her, "we shall walk past all my men and you will point out the one who was in your room."

Slowly, the general, Father, several officers and the maid marched between the rows of men.

The servant suddenly exclaimed, stopping in front of a rugged soldier, "This is the man."

"Were you in this woman's room?" demanded the general sternly.

The private did not answer; he stared straight ahead.

"Hold your arms out ahead of you," ordered the officer.

The soldier lifted his arms, and the general pulled back the sleeves of his tunic. Around both wrists were four or five watches.

"Is any one of these yours?" the commandant asked the maid.

"No," she replied.

The general bent down and lifted the soldier's pantleg. Two wrist watches were fastened around each ankle.

"That one is mine," the girl said, pointing.

The general, who was just back from riding his horse, lashed his crop unmercifully until the thief's face was raw and bloody. Then he turned towards the men. "This is a warning to all of you," he shouted. "Anyone caught stealing again will be shot." He turned and motioned Father to follow him back to the office.

"My men are from the front-line fighting and have long since forgotten the amenities of life," he explained. "Here they do many foolish and barbaric things. But you must forgive them. Today I have done all I could. I flogged one of my men as an example. But from now on—not a word of complaint from you or any of your people!"

From that day on, his soldiers behaved themselves.

A book could be written about the Russian occupation of our country. The Soviet soldiers were rough, naïve and primitive, yet they were touchingly good to the Czech children. They played with the youngsters, fondled them and plied them with sweets, which were at the time available only on the black market.

After being in our country for six months, the men were ordered back to Russia before Christmas. This was evidently distasteful to many who liked Czechoslovakia and wanted to settle permanently within our boundaries. The Reds had no pity for defectors and these young soldiers were naturally in danger of capture. They were in constant trouble, for their possessions were limited to army uniforms and gear, which were easily spotted. So they improvised. After dark, they would skulk in pairs in the shadow of a building or an alley until a well dressed citizen passed by. Then they would pounce, drag him to a secret spot and strip him of his clothes which they would substitute for their uniforms. In those days, it was not uncommon to see a man in his underwear sprinting home.

The effect of our Russian visitation can be summed up in the reply of our late president, Dr. Eduard Benes, given in answer to a question on whether he thought Czechoslovakia could survive a third World War.

"Yes, Czechoslovakia could survive a third World War," he said, "but not another Russian liberation."

Freedom returned to our country. Life in many ways went on as it had before the war. People began to recover from the physical and mental strain the hostilities had imposed on them.

For our family, too, there was a semblance of the old comfortable routine. Father's business began to prosper. But he was not deluded by the surface placidity.

"The Communists will soon rule our country," he prophesied to his business friends. "Let's not get caught by them as we were by the Nazis. It might be wise to put money in Swiss or English banks, in case industry becomes nationalized. We must be ready to leave without delay if the Communists take over."

His friends laughed at his dour warning. Who could believe that a democratic country like Czechoslovakia could turn Bolshevik? The thought was ridiculous!

Nevertheless, Father quietly opened bank accounts in Switzerland and England.

Our parents also sent Frank to a Swiss boarding school to learn foreign languages, while Richard attended a French school in

Prague. I was still under kindergarten age, but Maria and Otto already went to school.

They missed Frank. They not only respected their eldest brother but looked up to him. And Frank graciously accepted their adoration and services. Maria brought Frank his breakfast tray Saturdays and Sundays, and it was a loving act she was to continue whenever Frank was at home until he married. She also was allowed to polish his shoes, a task at which she worked arduously, for Frank was never satisfied unless the leather was mirror-smooth. Perhaps her compulsion for endless practice on skates stems from the work she put in on Frank's boots.

In April 1947, Otto and Maria gave their first figure skating show at the Winter Stadium in Prague. They jumped the gun, however. Fifteen minutes before the carnival was to commence, while spectators were still filing in to their seats, Otto decided he and Maria had waited backstage long enough for their turn. Suddenly, he grabbed Maria by the hand and pulled her out on the ice. Although the show had not yet started, they began their routine. Mother, Father and their skating instructor tried desperately to wave them back. But to no avail.

Since no music was playing, Otto began to sing loudly and they glided in rhythm to his tune. At the end of their routine, they bowed and left the ice. The applause they received for their public debut was tremendous.

Our parents were also listed on the program. They skated in a dance number with five other couples. Throughout their performance, Father, dressed in formal evening attire, kept tripping awkwardly. One of his skate laces had come undone. Finally, he flattened out on the ice, spraining his ankle in the fall. Mother kept on dancing alone, glancing repeatedly over her shoulder to see if Father would get up. Unable to rise because of his injured foot, Father crawled slowly towards the stage-curtain, much to the amusement of the crowd. All the spotlights were focused on him, and despite his pain, he managed to rise to his feet and bow deeply to the spectators. He received a spectacular ovation.

It was the habit of our parents, since the first year of their marriage, to attend the winter Olympics. The 1948 Olympics were held in St. Moritz, a story-book ski resort high in the glittering

Swiss Alps. Approximately a week later, the World Championships were scheduled for Davos.

The warm sun reflected its glory on the large natural rink and
dazzled the crowd with its splinters of gold. There were the skiing
and skating contests. Our parents, as usual, were particularly
affected by the magnificent display of skating skills. First, there
were the Pairs; then the men skaters, with Dick Button, superb
and deserving of his title, and then the girl skaters. The audience
was tense as Barbara Ann Scott, the great Canadian skater who
was then at the peak of her ability, stepped on the ice. She was
an enchanting, freckle-faced eighteen-year-old, dressed in white
and silver lamé. Her costume combined with her slim figure and
golden hair gave her the appearance of a princess in a Pogany
painting.

Barbara Ann was unbelievable; the crowd was stunned by the
skill and beauty of her performance. Mother whispered, "If only
one of our children could some day skate like that." Father smiled
beneficently at her. Her happiness gave him great pleasure. But
before he could answer, someone tapped him on the shoulder. He
looked up to see a man standing beside him.

"Oh, hello, Carl . . ." Father broke off abruptly, startled by the
strained anxious look on his friend's face. "Whatever is the
matter?"

The friend motioned Father to follow him.

"I'll be right back, dear," Father said to Mother. But she was
still too absorbed watching Barbara Ann to heed his words.

Carl was usually a jolly fellow; many of his friends called him
"Smiley" since he was always in a good mood. Today, however,
his face was tense. He spoke slowly as if searching for words.

"Are your children home?" he finally asked.

"Of course. They are in school. Why, has something happened?"

"Five minutes ago I phoned my secretary in Prague," Carl
interrupted. "Something tragic has happened." He repeated in
pained, jerky half sentences, tears coursing down his cheeks, the
news that had just come to him.

How can I possibly tell Jara? Father thought. Walking back to
his rink-side seat he seemed in a trance. What can I say to her?
Now, when she is so happy. I knew it would come. I knew it. But
that it should come now—so soon!

He sat glum and perturbed as the skaters swirled in what remained of the competition. It was a beautiful enthralling spectacle. Mother was still so enraptured that she did not notice Father's change of mood. It was only when they were back in their hotel room that she recognized his distress and agitation.

"Do you feel all right?" she asked anxiously. Then he gave her the news, blurting it out, powerless to soften its impact.

"Jara, the Communists have taken over our country." He had to repeat it before Mother could grasp its horrible meaning. She listened in stunned silence. Her lips moved, but words would not come.

First the German butchers. Now the Communists, imposing harsh, alien rule. For a second time, the country was to be put in captivity. Only those who have themselves been victims in a captive State can understand the anguish of my parents.

Finally, the shock eased somewhat and they embarked on the first of many long conversations, all having the single theme, "Whatever shall we do?"

The immediate plan, however, seemed clear enough.

"I'll go back home first thing in the morning, and see how I can get the children out of the country," Father said. "You go to stay with Frank at the school in Lausanne for the time being—and don't worry! Everything will be all right!" The assurance was assumed for Mother's benefit. He knew that the factory and probably our home as well, would be among the first properties confiscated by the Red government. But his grief was not limited by the prospect of personal deprivation. He knew that for Czechoslovakia it would mean a tragic farewell to freedom. There would be swift and perhaps permanent economic disaster. The price of bread would soar. The famous Czech industries, steel, glass, coal, ammunition, machine guns, would be seized by the State, ostensibly in the name of the people. Priority would henceforth be given to the needs of the Red Army.

How would the Jelinek staff be affected?

Our family cork factory was destined for prompt confiscation. By the time Father returned the next day to Prague, nationalization was already in effect. The more than two hundred workers on the Jelinek payroll were politically for the Communists. However, since Father had always been fair with them, they were reluctant to have him replaced by a Communist official, who might be less considerate of their needs. Accordingly, they tried to persuade Communist Party officials to nominate Father as the "new" manager of his own factory, which was now State property. Since the workers were so enthusiastic, the officials decided, reluctantly, to recommend Father to the Ministry of Industry and Commerce.

Thus, the "February events" had a shattering effect on the Jelineks, and the ice was thin again.

The "February events" soon brought their destruction to all the workers of Czechoslovakia. Privately owned industry was confiscated by the State officials. These lawless acts were carried out sanctimoniously in the name of the workers, who were ostensibly the new owners of the factories. In theory, this was an act of vindication for the proletariat. In practice, it meant something quite different, silent acceptance of the harsh rules of workshop management, designed to increase output without monetary rewards. Workers automatically lost the right to protest. Before the Red takeover, the workers had the right to strike and on occasion exercised that right. Now, it was forbidden. Let a worker even whisper the word, and if he were reported, it could easily mean prison for him. New regulations demanded that each worker donate an extra shift every other Sunday; this shift, ironically, was termed "voluntary."

Little of the Czech ordeal seemed to make a deep impression on the outer world, until the sudden death of Jan Masaryk.

"Young Masaryk," as he was admiringly known to millions, was the surviving son of the great Thomas Masaryk who, when the Republic of Czechoslovakia was set up in 1918, became its first president. The Reds kept young Masaryk on after the "February events." He was useful to their propaganda. He figured in their Cabinet as a non-party Foreign Minister, which gave the regime a façade of respectability. The Reds hoped that the West's reaction to their rape of the country would be mitigated by Masaryk's acceptance of an official role in the regime.

All Prague wondered what really went on in Jan Masaryk's mind. Did he go along with the Reds in their thinking, or did he feel it his duty to remain in his country? His father had been idealized as the Liberator. Did young Jan see himself in the role of a Mediator? Did he finally realize his hopes were unrealistic and take his own life? Or did the Prague Reds receive orders from Russia to liquidate him?

No one will ever know the truth. For Jan was found dead early one morning in the courtyard of the Foreign Office building in Prague. The lights were still burning in his apartment, three stories above the courtyard. His window was wide open.

The evidence pointed to suicide. This was the official version which none of Prague gave credence to. Yet there was a sense of irony even in the calculated report, for Masaryk the Elder had achieved his academic distinction by writing a philosophic thesis on suicide.

The senior Masaryk was Father's idol, and we children were brought up to revere his memory much as our American contemporaries revere Lincoln. Thomas Garrigue Masaryk, who was to become our noted statesman, wrote his book on suicide when he was twenty-one years old. Within ten years, he was appointed Professor of Philosophy at the University of Prague. He became the voice of the Czech minority in the Austro-Hungarian Parliament in Vienna. He foresaw the crackup of the Hapsburg monarchy. He foresaw the emergence of an independent Czechoslovakia as the result of a future war. Shortly after World War I started, he escaped from Prague and reached Switzerland. He wandered through Europe and finally arrived in the United States. It was in Philadelphia that he published, on the eve of the breakup of the Austro-Hungarian empire, and Czechoslovakia's emergence as a sovereign state, the famous "Declaration of Independence." There was a striking similarity in concept between his declaration and the one which made the thirteen American states a democracy.

Masaryk's valiant stand was rewarded by his election as President of Czechoslovakia. The Old Man's skill in statecraft was largely inherited by his son, Jan. But many of his compatriots wondered if the son had also inherited the father's vigor and singleness of purpose.

Rumors abounded in Prague about Jan's death. There is no official verification, but this story was widely accepted in our country as the truth about Jan Masaryk's end.

Late in the afternoon of March 9, 1948, a black sedan stopped at the main entrance of the ancient Hradcany castle. From the back seat emerged a tall, heavyset man, hatless and in a loose tweed coat, the collar up around his neck. He entered the edifice which since 1918 had been the residence of the President of the Republic of Czechoslovakia. He walked quickly down the corridor and stopped before a huge scrolled door.

The President was waiting for him in the library.

Masaryk found Benes slumped in an armchair before the fireplace in the library. Benes was weary and disheveled; a listless air had usurped the vigor of the once energetic leader.

It is rumored that Jan Masaryk said to President Benes, "Eduard, I am leaving tonight for London." He is thought to have told Benes that he knew *they* were after him. And Benes, bone weary, defeated, agreed with his decision. Neither of them could help their people, for Benes and Masaryk were the only two non-Communists left in the government which had been formed ten days previously after the Communist riot. Both men were being watched by the Russian secret police. Jan Masaryk, especially, was a target for their suspicions, since he had been a leading member of the democratic government for two decades and was extremely popular with the people.

So, it is said, the two men parted in sorrow, knowing they wouldn't meet again. When Masaryk returned to his office in the Department of External Affairs, it is supposed that Dr. Clementis was waiting to see him. Clementis, Masaryk's deputy minister, was an avowed Communist. Masaryk accepted an invitation for dinner the following evening with the new Swedish minister which Clementis was to arrange, and then abruptly dismissed the fellow.

With the help of his secretary, Masaryk destroyed all of his correspondence in the fireplace. The secretary, Miss Maria Firt, who was to accompany Masaryk to London, was one of the few people to know of his plan.

At five o'clock on the morning of March 10, Jan's body was found under the window of his bedroom, three stories above. The body was examined by his personal physician, who certified that death was caused from injuries sustained by a fall from a great height.

MASARYK COMMITS SUICIDE! the headlines screamed. Throughout Prague, people gathered in hushed groups, too shocked and grieved to speculate on what might have happened. One thing, however, seemed a fact to most of them: it did not seem possible that a man of Jan Masaryk's energy and humor and zest for life could have killed himself.

His body lay in state in the castle. The Czechs paid their last tribute to their beloved Jan Masaryk. Their tears were not only for him but for the death of their hopes.

They say—

They say—

They say that a Comrade reported to Stalin that his mission in Prague was completed.

They say that the gunman from the Kremlin dined with Clementis on the evening of March 9, and they came to the conclusion that it would be difficult to get rid of Masaryk without arousing the ire of the populace.

They say that the gunman met Klement Gottwald, who was Prime Minister of Czechoslovakia, and that Gottwald reported Masaryk was about to flee the country. Then, it is rumored, Gottwald, Clementis and the gunman took off for the airport, where they found Masaryk already in the plane, waiting for the takeoff. He was accompanied by his assistant and his secretary. Gottwald is supposed to have ordered him to cancel the trip to London, and Masaryk refused. With extraordinary self-possession and pride, he turned his back on the three men. It was then that the assassin from the Kremlin drew his gun, levelled it at the back of Masaryk's head, squeezed the trigger twice. Jan Masaryk crumpled to the floor.

At the sound of the shots, the plane's crew of two rushed in. But Clementis, interpreting the gunman's orders, warned the crew and Masaryk's staff to be silent about what had happened. It was simple enough to remove Masaryk's body from the plane and take it to his apartment, where it was shoved through the open window to crash on the stones below.

In the five days before the state funeral, Masaryk's secretary, his assistant, and his doctor all disappeared. Nothing was ever heard from them again.

This is the story that leaped like fire from tongue to tongue in Prague during that perilous time. The truth will probably never be known, but Father and many of his friends believe this to be the true story.

A fortnight after Masaryk's death, farmers working in the fields of Domazlice, a quiet village near the German border of Czechoslovakia, were witness to the landing of a small United States Air Force plane.

"They are here. They have come at last!" cried the farmers. Ploughs abandonded, they sprinted to the village, shouting the glorious news that Americans had arrived to liberate them from the Communists. The villagers raided the local jail. Overpowering the guards, they freed political prisoners. Then they jailed all the Communist officials in the district. Finally, unable to contain their joy, they started a spontaneous celebration in the village square. The population laughed and wept with joy.

"We are free!" The happy shout echoed in the square. "We have been rescued!"

But suddenly, they realized that something was not quite right. Several trucks of Communist police from nearby Pilsen charged into the square. The Americans were in their midst. Then the villagers were shattered by the news. The Americans had made a forced landing. They were not the vanguard of an invasion for freedom. They were just two fliers who had the bad luck to have trouble with their engine. Now they were prisoners of the Communists. Heaven only knew what would happen to them.

Whereupon the Communists rounded up the political prisoners and imprisoned them again, adding the villagers who were so clearly anti-Communist. The action of the villagers was an indication of the secret hopes of millions of Czechs. After the death of Masaryk, a single flame of hope burned in their hearts.

The hope of an American liberation.

For this they waited.

And they still wait.

But many have given up hope.

chapter six

W͟ITH MASARYK'S DEATH, HOPES OF ACTIVE
intervention from the West died. Prague was in a shock of mourning. Then, one day, Father was ordered to report to the Ministry
of Industry and Commerce.

The official was polite, even smiling, which promised a disagreeable session for Father.

"Do sit down, Mr. Jelinek."

"Thank you." Father obeyed.

The Minister began on an unctuous note. "You are extremely
fortunate, Mr. Jelinek. May I congratulate you on your new
position."

Father's brows lifted in surprise.

"Did you not know of it? You are now not only manager of our
cork factory, but chief buyer for the entire bottle-cap and cork
industry of Czechoslovakia." He paused delicately. "I take it you
are willing to accept the appointment?"

"Certainly." Father's philosophy was expediency; agree with
your adversary in all the small matters that precede the real crisis.

"We are prepared to issue you a passport," the Minister said.

This bit of news startled Father. For when the Communists
grabbed power, they issued an emergency decree that voided all
passports except those endorsed as "valid only for journeys vital
to the State."

This was one of their tricks for trapping on the frontiers those of their victims who sought safety in flight. The Minister added shrewdly, "Armed with this passport, you will be able to leave the country at any time. Now, when you go abroad, your task will be to set up barter deals between our trading organization and other nations."

Father could scarcely conceal the effect of his good fortune. It was a fantastic offer. A passport for him, endorsed by the Red rulers and valid for crossing the frontier? Could it be a genuine offer, or was there a concealed trick to it?

"Of course," the Minister added, "your wife must return from Switzerland before we issue your passport."

Father's heart lurched; his hopes were cruelly shattered. He was sick with disappointment. So it was the old trick, holding a member of the family as a hostage. How similar was the thinking of the Nazis and the Reds!

For this agonizing quandary, Father had no ready solution. Yet he was never one to give up easily. He played along with the Minister. He pretended interest in the opportunities afforded him in his new post. He even managed to ignore the fact that it was his own factory he would be representing for the gains of his enemies. He did his best to consider the plus factors in the deal. Fortunately, Father had lost neither his courage nor his optimism. They flickered once in a while, but like a candle wavering in the wind, they never were completely snuffed out. It was unthinkable to Father that the God he cherished should deny him the right to save his family. If God wanted him to use his wits, he was prepared to comply.

At least, he reflected, this meant he still had some freedom left. Freedom to exercise his brains in search of a means of escape for his family.

Most of the actual owners of factories vital to the new State's industrial program—the output of weapons for the eastern armies and engines for the friends of the Kremlin—were either in prison or, at best, employed in the most menial tasks in their own businesses.

Father therefore had no illusions about the official Red aims for him. He was clearly of great value to the new rulers of Czechoslovakia—at least for the time being—until they trained their own party apprentices in the branch of industry that he knew so well. Relatively few in Czechoslovakia really understood the finer points of the cork industry. The Communists were bound to keep Father, in one capacity or another, until his usefulness was exhausted.

This was fortunate for the family. It gave him extra time to search for an escape route for us five Jelineks. Friends of ours who with typical Czech optimism had tried to arrange for their own escape found that there was a rude limit to Communist reasonableness. For Father there was also the realization that any attempt to flee across the border with a group of small children was too risky to attempt. So a frontier dash across hills and forests in the dark night was ruled out for us.

But a scheme was decided on. Not the perfect method of escape but one that seemed to involve the fewest possible risks.

At this point, a South American diplomat enters the picture, prominent but anonymous. For it was part of our compact with him that he should never be identified. We will call him, simply, "Mr. G."

A shadowy coffee bar in a narrow side street of downtown Prague became a secret meeting place. Here Mr. G. sat facing Father across a table littered with soggy beer mats. The two had reached the final stage of their discussions. On Mr. G.'s part, this involved the dollars he would get. His price, like the price of bread under the Communists, showed an alarming tendency to soar.

Mr. G. addressed Father. "Senor," he said in his somewhat weird Czech, marked by a strong Spanish accent, "I am prepared to undertake the risk of getting your wife with your three children out of the country." He smiled drily. "For a little bag of money, as I have said. In dollars, of course."

Not so little, thought Father grimly. But his mind that day was mainly on his children. "But Mr. G., there are five children in our family. One is safely out of the country, in school in Switzerland. As for the others, the last thing I would agree to is the split-up of the family. Whatever happens, our family stays together."

The diplomat showed traces of nerves.

"I don't think you quite realize, Senor, how difficult it would be for me to arrange a successful escape for all of your family at once.

"Along most Czech borders, Communist guards have cut out a

'death swath' about a mile wide. They've chopped down trees and
flattened the terrain of all undergrowth. They've put up barbed
wire fences, made 'live' by strong currents of electricity. Nobody
can get through that way. Police dogs working in squads with
armed soldiers patrol day and night. Search lights play over the
entire area. How could you hope to get clear anywhere?"

The consul paused, betraying his tension as he lit one of
Father's cigarettes. "Hundreds of people have been shot trying to
escape."

Father was not deterred by the way the talk was going. Calmly
he replied, "You know I will pay you very well." Thus he indicated to the diplomat that the accepted price for the fugitive
enterprise had taken another upward leap.

Mr. G.'s misgivings continued. "I beg of you to appreciate,
Senor, the great risk I am taking. I would remind you that the
plan to use my own passport for myself, and that of my wife and
three children for Mrs. Jelinek and your children is highly dangerous. The photo in my family's passport is my wife's. I am sure
Mrs. Jelinek looks nothing like her. The names of our children
are written on her passport. But there are only three of them and
there are four of yours. If you really want to take the fearful
risk . . ." He paused, then he shrugged. "Very well, Senor, I will
take that extra chance. Pray God that we get them past the frontier
guards."

"I do not underestimate the enormous risks involved," said
Father. "We are willing to face them."

The two men, heads conspiratorially close, rehearsed the details
once again: the hour of rendezvous, the exact timing along the
route. The risk of their being overheard and reported was very
real. But since this risk seemed so negligible compared with the
hazards involved in the actual escape, neither man fretted over it.

For Father this was zero hour. All had to be arranged at that
final meeting with Mr. G. Armed with his new Communist-
sponsored passport, Father was due to leave Prague the following
day on the first business assignment which the Czech Ministry of
Industry had entrusted to him. The Communists, convinced they
could be sure of him now that Mother had dutifully returned to
the country, had actually agreed to lend him a car. The car had

originally been his own, until "in the name of the people," he had been forced to turn it over to the State.

Only our grandmother Zizka knew we hoped to escape from our country. For relatives, friends and servants, our story was that Mother was in the need of relaxation, and so she was taking the children to the country for the weekend. We had to make sure that all of us told the same story. In those days, you were never certain who, among friends and servants, had secretly turned Communist and would report you to the authorities.

Even after our plans for escape were complete, with every contingency allowed for, there came a delay of almost two weeks before the perilous adventure could begin. The South American diplomat kept changing his mind. He was nervous. More people were being caught every day in the flight to the frontier. The border guards were trigger-happy. Those refugees who escaped bullets were promptly jailed and faced a future of inquisition and torture.

That was the perilous situation which faced Mother. Imagine her dilemma as one day Otto reminded her he would be eight next week, and would he be allowed to choose the bicycle promised for his birthday?

Mother begged Otto to be a good sport about it. The promise was not forgotten. But first they would take a trip to the country. Otto insisted, in childish stubbornness, that bicycle-choosing must have top priority.

In Switzerland, meanwhile, Father was waiting to get his wife, sons and daughter out of the Reds' clutches. Made more nervous by the impatient questions of his oldest son, Frank ("when will they get here"), he took a calculated risk and telephoned home from Lausanne. He knew that the Secret Police were tapping all calls from outside Czechoslovakia. Therefore, he and Mother spoke according to a prearranged code. To an alert agent, however, the code would have presented no difficulties.

First came the genuine questions. "How are you, Jara, and how are the children? What's the weather like? We've had another bright and sunny day here."

Then Father switched over to the scrambler: "By the way, how is the dressmaker coming along with your new outfit?" (Meaning: "Where have you got to with your escape plans?")

Mother answered, "She still has a few buttons to sew on, but I think it should definitely be completed within five days."

"Perhaps you should tell her to stop work on it," Father commented. "In which case, I could bring a new dress home for you."

His suggestion paralyzed Mother; she took it to mean he was seriously considering giving up the project and coming back to the perils of the Home Front.

"Oh, no!" In her acute distress, she nearly gave herself away. "Don't let's give up now."

On May 14, 1948, there was a secret last minute meeting between Mr. G. and Mother.

"This time, it's definite," he announced. "Tomorrow, I drive you all to the border and out of the country."

Our Otto, irrepressible and impudent, nearly gave the whole plan away. After being scolded by his teacher, he retorted, "You needn't fuss. Pretty soon, I'll be leaving this beastly school forever."

When he proudly reported this conversation to Mother, she nearly fainted with shock. Actually, Otto had no idea of the plans taking shape for our flight. It was merely an exercise in bravado. But Mother feared that his fanciful ultimatum could arouse the teacher's suspicions and send the Secret Police on our trail.

May 15; 4:30 A.M. Mother spent an anxious, sleepless night going through our scant bits of luggage to make doubly sure they yielded no clue to an intention of permanent departure. Then she woke us.

"We're leaving almost at once. The taxi will be here to take us to the station in fifteen minutes."

Mr. G. the diplomat had refused to take the risk of calling for us at the house. He assumed it would be watched by police.

4:45 A.M. Headlights swept up the driveway. Mother held her breath. But it was not the police, only the taxi, prompt on the dot, as the driver had promised.

We climbed sleepily into the taxi. Grandmother Zizka, up six hours earlier than usual to see us off, began crying. I couldn't figure out why. After all, we were only going off to the country for a day or two. "We'll soon be back, Grandmother," I said, "so please, don't cry."

None of us ever saw her again.

Richard, just turned eleven, knew of the plans so he had guessed what was going on. Mother, thinking it was better that way, entrusted him with the secret. She simply had to share it with some one, and although it was a tremendous responsibility with which to burden a young boy, she felt that Richard would accept it bravely.

At the station, we descended; Mother paid the driver. A large sedan was parked off to one side. Hesitantly Mother herded us toward it. Suddenly, there was a sound of footsteps behind us. Mother thought in panic, So they did follow us, after all. But she maintained her composure, and a moment later, Mr. G.'s voice spoke softly in her ear.

"Get in, all of you. Quickly! We must be on our way at once."

His car was ample for the four of us children and Mother. Once we were on the road, Mother said, "Children, let us play a little game. Let's pretend this gentleman driving the car is your father. Yes, I do think it's a good idea. Now, if anyone should stop us and ask who he is, what will you say?"

We were all silent. Somehow the game didn't appeal to us.

"You will say, 'He is my daddy,' " Mother prompted us.

Only Richard pretended to be enthusiastic. The tension of the elders communicated itself somehow to us children.

"We're being followed!" the diplomat cried, terrified after several minutes of driving. He saw the reflection of headlights in the rear-view mirror. "See if you can make out who it is," he demanded hoarsely.

But as Mother turned in her seat, she saw Richard's wide, frightened eyes. He was trembling for he knew we were courting disaster. Mother forced herself to look beyond him, just as the headlights of the following car veered off the main road.

"It's nobody, after all," she said. We children sensed her relief. But it was brief. Her tensions mounted as we drove towards the border. Six hours passed; for us children they proved to be un-eventful, even boring hours. But for Mother, they must have been a truly grim ordeal. Mother is by temperament, and even in tranquil times, a world champion worrier. For her, the ice is eternally thin under the feet of all her kin. She has never really liked to have any one of her children undertake big-time skating too far from home. With them near at hand, as Mother has often announced quite seriously, she knows exactly at what hour they will be on the ice. She knows exactly, therefore, at what hour to turn on the worry tap. But when the family skaters find themselves on the far side of a time meridian, involving a change in time, Mother is distressed. Having the European background of relatively small distances, she never knows exactly what time it is anywhere but near home. How can she, therefore, be sure of when she ought to start being anxious. Thus, a new worry is born.

Maria and Otto, and perhaps to a lesser degree, Frank, Richard and I, have been conditioned to a similar reaction. We all worry, but in different degrees. We are nevertheless all sensitive to the fact that our parents worry a good deal about us. They have a right to, considering what they have suffered to keep the family intact. Lesser characters might have broken down.

However, during that dash to freedom, it was only Mother who was fraught with anxiety. For us young ones, it was just tedious and unending.

Abruptly, Mr. G. announced, "I must stop for gas."

Just three more miles to the border and he was looking for a gas station. Couldn't he make it to the border?

"Impossible," he said. Then, as he braked the car, a Communist policeman with a rifle slung over his shoulder approached us. "Oh, dear God!" Mr. G.'s voice was trembling.

"Mommy," Maria interrupted in her piping voice, "When will we see Daddy again?"

Mother saw the policeman motion to the diplomat, who was being ordered to lower his window. She whispered to us children. "Be quiet now, and do remember our game. We are pretending this is Daddy with us."

The guard asked brusquely, "Where are you going?"

"To Austria," Mr. G. replied.

The guard peered into the rear windows. Maria smiled at him. She announced, "This is our daddy."

"Oh? So you are one family?"

"Yes, yes," said Mr. G. quickly. Maria giggled.

"Give me a lift to the border," the Communist ordered. He climbed into the back seat. The children edged closer to one another.

"What are the children doing out of school today?" asked the unwelcome guest.

"They go to a French school in Prague," Mother said quickly. "They have no school today and we will be back on Monday."

"Oh, so they speak French," said the policeman. "Parlez-vous Français?" he asked.

Mother knew French fluently, Richard almost fluently, since he attended a French school.

"Oui," Richard responded, lips trembling with the enormous fears of childhood.

The Communist seemed satisfied. At least he showed no overt suspicions. Sitting beside him, Otto played with the guard's rifle. This amused the policeman, but Mother fretted for fear Otto might become too friendly and in his innocent chatter betray us all.

"Stop it," she told Otto. The policeman looked at her sternly.

"Are you a Czech or a Communist?" asked Otto, startling the policeman as well as Mother and the diplomat.

"We are all Communists," the man answered gruffly. "Hurry it up," he said to Mr. G. The diplomat obligingly stepped on the gas pedal. He was only too anxious to have the journey ended.

"Dad lets me play with his gun," was the irrepressible Otto's next statement. "If he were here . . ."

"You just sit back and don't say another word," said Mother quickly in a tone that warned Otto to obey. Then to change the subject she feigned a smile and asked Mr. G., "Tell me, dear, how soon will we reach the border?"

"Any time, now," replied the diplomat, glancing at Mother sitting beside him and remembering to add under the rules of our game, the words, "my dear."

Both their faces betrayed strain. But the policeman, who by this time seemed equally anxious to reach journey's end, noticed nothing. He stared moodily out of the window. Landmarks along the thick evergreen forest which the road bisected assured Mother, who had travelled this route often in happier days, that the border region was approaching.

All of a sudden we were there. On the right stood a small hut —the customs house.

The policeman jumped out of the car and waved to the two border guards standing beside the heavy steel barrier which blocked our road to freedom. He hurried to the gate and changed places with one of the guards, leaving us all in the car. The man off-duty drove away on a motor scooter, while the large dogs tied to a cable next to the road, started barking viciously.

"I'm scared, Mommy," cried Maria.

"Nothing to be frightened of," Mother assured her, pretending a calm she was far from feeling.

The door of the hut opened. Another guard motioned for the diplomat. "Here we go," Mr. G. muttered as he climbed out of the car. He entered the small office. Five or six uniformed Communists were lounging in the room. The quizzing began.

"What is your name?" asked a heavy-set man leaning against the wall.

"Alex G., accredited consul general of ———," he replied. Before he could mention the name of his country, he was rudely interrupted.

"Where are you going?"

"To Austria, for the weekend."

"Is that your family out there?" the man asked, pointing towards the road.

"Yes."

"Give me your papers!" ordered the officer.

Mr. G. handed him the passport. The guard looked at it closely, though it was in Spanish, and then asked, "How many of you are there?"

"Five," answered the consul, losing what small hope he had mustered. The passport was issued for five, but there were six of us.

"Joseph," the questioner addressed another guard by the door, "go and search the car and tell me how many there are."

"You have no right whatsoever to inspect my car," argued Mr. G. "It is a diplomatic automobile and under international law you are not allowed to search it."

"Joseph," the Communist ordered, ignoring the diplomat, "do as I say."

"We are caught now," thought Mother as the guard called Joseph approached the sedan, a rifle in his hand. All this scheming and planning for nothing. Failure at the very last fence.

"All out," he ordered roughly, waving his rifle to reinforce his order. At Mother's side of the car, he yanked the door open. Trying to stifle her fears, Mother said quickly, "Come, children, do as the man asks."

Bayonet on rifle, the guard jabbed under the seats, using his bayonet as a probe. Angry at finding nothing, he ordered us in again and stomped back to the shack.

"Well, how many are there?" the heavy-set man asked.

"Five," Joseph replied.

Counting those of us in the car, Joseph had forgotten to add the consul to the number. So five it was, as stated in the passport. Joseph probably saved our lives by his one figure oversight. But we were not yet through.

The chief guard stared down at the passport in his hand with a blank expression.

"Tell me what it says," he ordered Mr. G.

The diplomat translated, saying what he hoped would be appropriate for the occasion, knowing that actually none of the Communists was likely to understand Spanish.

"So your wife is from South America, too. I shall ask her a few questions."

As the guard strode out to the car, the consul, ashen and shaking, followed. Mother had opened her window, aware of trouble brewing. But her face was miraculously composed.

"You speak Spanish?" the chief guard asked curtly.

Mother smiled blandly. "Si, si," she said, exhausting her vocabulary.

"Very well, translate this page of the passport," he ordered.

Mother's pulse accelerated. What was she to do? Puzzled, helpless, she stared at the Communist. But Mr. G. came to her rescue with an adroit answer.

"Sir, my wife doesn't speak Czech," he said. This was a calculated risk, since the Communist to whom he had given a lift was standing only a few yards away. Had he heard? Mother wondered. Dear God, could he have heard?

chapter seven

Meanwhile, Father and Frank were waiting impatiently in Lausanne. Father, being acutely conscious of the risks to which his family was subjected, was sick with anxiety. But it was all held within. Frank saw only his confident, smiling autocratic parent.

"How soon will they come?" Frank asked again and again.

"Soon. Don't fret, son," Father calmed him, without actually being calm himself. In their coded phone conversation Mother had told him that they would escape at the latest within five days. It was now already the sixth. He kept this information from Frank, for he was much too aware of the risk involved in the flight and of the retaliations awaiting his family if they had the ill fortune to be caught. The thought of his family being taken captive made him physically ill. Although Father tried to appear calm his nervousness communicated itself to Frank. "Maybe it would be a good idea for you to go back to school," Father said. "I'll meet you at the hotel after classes." Frank was reluctant but finally agreed to leave, since he too felt that it might do him good.

After Frank's departure, Father started wandering aimlessly along the cobbled walks of Lausanne. He felt utterly helpless. His mind dwelt on the possible dangers. His thoughts exploded into a nightmare of horror. He paused and gazed down at the calm waters of Lake Geneva. Instead of his own reflection, however, he saw the image of our Mother, being roughly handled by the guards. And Maria, her cheeks moist with tears, crying as she was dragged into a prison; then Otto, his face frozen in terror . . . Suddenly the laughter of a small girl broke his horrible vision. Maria? No, it was not Maria, but another little girl with pigtails, a free girl, a safe girl calmly feeding the seagulls along the boardwalk.

Father was angry at himself for being so helpless. He was convinced that something had gone terribly wrong. Why not fly back to Prague and see what I can do? he thought. He decided that if his family didn't arrive today, he would return to Prague in the morning.

An hour passed. Father telephoned the hotel. No news. Another hour crawled by, then another and yet another. Still no news from his wife and children. Father walked back to the hotel. Frank joined him. They sat there gloomily, each buried with his own thoughts.

"I'll be right back, son," Father said to Frank.

He had made his decision.

He crossed the street in front of the hotel and entered the travel bureau where, in earlier days, he had made so many reservations for happy journeys. . . . Now with a sick heart he asked to make another reservation. Tomorrow he would return to Prague. All his hopes for a successful family escape had vanished. He was a ruined man. He had thought, as so many others had, that he could outsmart the communists. But he had lost.

On the hotel stairs he heard the sound of the concierge's voice, loud with excitement, "Here they come."

"Here they come!"

But how many? Would all five members of his family arrive safely on a passport which was not legally theirs and which provided only for four people?

Suppose the Red Czechs had held one of us for a hostage? That would spell not only the end of freedom for us all but possible death. So Father rushed out into the courtyard of the hotel, his husky voice thick with emotion.

"How many?" he asked.

A bellboy shouted, "Many, many! A whole car full!"

But that was not enough for Father; now the perspiration

fogged his eyes; his hands as well as his eyes were counting, as we emerged from the car.

One; two; three; four; and Mama.

And Mr. G., who having collected his own form of ransom, swiftly managed to lose himself.

In the hotel suite, there was the joyous bedlam of reunion.

"How lucky we are," Mother said, crying and laughing simultaneously, "that one guard could not count and another was half deaf. Oh! and poor little Maria. After I told her we had escaped she said, 'But Mommy, we must return, I forgot my dolls.' "

Richard was helping Mother unpack the scanty luggage that Mr. G. had decided was ample for our so-called weekend in Austria. Otto was roughhousing with Maria and myself. When Father entered the suite, having made arrangements with the front desk, which he had not dared to make until our actual arrival, Otto said casually, "Hello, Father," as though we had been apart from Father for a few minutes instead of endless days. Father kissed us all, and said quietly, "From now on, wherever we go, we go together; whatever we do, we do together."

This philosophy was the heartwarming stuff that was to bind us together in the face of difficulties we had yet to encounter. The sense of unity, born that moment, has become a part of our lives. By vision, by will, by sheer determination, Father kept us together and preserved us against odds that could easily have destroyed us. He had proved in the Nazi prison that faith can overcome fear; in a hundred ways, he has demonstrated it since then. When a critical situation is not frozen by fright, and man can act with courage, that courage seems to ignite the most extraordinary latent forces within him, bringing out strength and ingenuity to vanquish the destructive obstacles. Father never let us forget that God has made man to be free. We absorbed his unwavering faith by osmosis. Since he has proved his faith works, we have accepted it without reserve. It has turned exile into home; it has held us fast in times of trouble and is always the source of our good fortune.

I know that in America a dynamic Father image is sometimes questioned; that psychiatrists bemoan the effect of a patriarchal parent on his children. But in our case, there is no doubt in our minds, that Father's strength, no matter how trying it appeared at times to us, was our saving grace in our ordeal. Since then, there are times when we question his orders, but in those days of trouble, when our future rested on a Red whim of chance, we obeyed unquestioningly. We have never since regretted it. He's quite a man, our father, and we revere him while we tease and badger him.

Shortly after we were safe in Switzerland, Father wrote to the Communist who was chairman of our former factory and asked that his letter be read to the entire personnel. He was doubtful whether his request would be granted but this was the only way that he knew to communicate with his old staff and inform them of his feelings.

He wrote: "I am indeed sorry to have to inform you that, after thoroughly considering all the existing circumstances, I have decided to resign from the position of manager of my former factory and not to return to Czechoslovakia under the current conditions.

"My decision to take this vital and drastic step was influenced by the following logic:

"1) Due to the planning of the new regime, the state of the economy in our country is rapidly deteriorating, and I do not wish to witness the downfall of the enterprise for which I have worked and lived.

"2) My guiding principle—to reward my staff well above normal level—is well known. Under the new regime, wages and salaries are fixed and considerably decreased. I refuse to remain an impotent bystander while there is a gradual decline in the living standards of my faithful employees.

"3) At the start of the war, we were forced from our home by the Germans. Now, once again, this senseless act has been repeated by another invader. My home has been confiscated. I have been ordered out, with no provisions to accommodate my family. The Peoples' Democratic Government is in possession of my home and furnishings.

"There will be a few trouble makers among my personnel who will cry out that I absconded with a State automobile. The irony is that the car is my own. It was part of my fortune which has been all nationalized. Some of the prominent Communists have promised that I would be reimbursed for the takeover of my belongings. If this should ever happen, I am quite willing to have them deduct the price of the car from the total estate. The sum will be infinitesimal.

"I ask understanding of those of my friends and staff who know me. This has not been an easy decision on my part, but appears to be the only alternative left to us.

"You are all very dear to me, and I take leave of you with a broken heart and with the wish for the best for you and your families in this new confused world."

Was this message ever given to the staff?

Not by the Communists. But later, through the Underground, we heard that every one of Father's workers did read it. The girls in the office made copies and secretly passed them out. Our old chauffeur took copies to Father's friends. It was circulated inside the factory and out, and finally reprinted and distributed as a leaflet by the Underground.

Father had said the world had become confusing. Yet for us, after a while, life resumed a facsimile of a normal pattern. We settled down to the interim as temporary residents in Switzerland. Richard, Otto, Maria and I were enrolled in Frank's school. Frank and Richard hankered to become top ice hockey players. The rest of us concentrated on figure skating. Mother learned to enjoy shopping in French.

We were all in reasonably good spirits and superb health, except for Father. Now that we were all safe, the physical effects of his jousting with the Communists made itself evident. The stomach pains he had tried so long to ignore finally worsened. The doctor's verdict was blunt. Father entered the hospital for an ulcer operation. If his spirits wavered, there was no evidence of it during his convalescence. He bullied the nurses, and they adored him. His surgeon saw through the gruff gallantry and refused to send him a bill.

"You are an emigré with a large family," the doctor said. "I know you will need every cent to rehabilitate yourself."

There was no bill. This became something of a hassle between Father's fierce pride and the doctor's practical good sense. They finally compromised by a bouquet of red roses for the surgeon's wife. But Father never forgot and several hospitals' wings have

benefited by the doctor's gracious gesture to a desperately sick
refugee.

It was in Switzerland that the Jelinek family unit first showed itself on ice. All seven of us appeared in a simple unpretentious ice
show put on by the combined skating clubs of Lausanne.

We were introduced by the master of ceremonies as a family
who had recently fled from Communist Czechoslovakia. The spotlights shone on us, all seven dressed alike, the tallest, Frank, on the
right, grading down to the smallest—myself, at the left. We
marched to the music of "The Stars and Stripes Forever" to the far
end of the arena. Here Father and Mother paired off, as did Otto
and Maria. They skated in couples, attempting difficult lifts that
neither our parents or brother and sister could manage properly,
since one couple was too old and the other too young. Meanwhile,
Frank, Richard and I managed a few fancy steps and bungled
several jumps. At the end of our program, we marched off the ice.
Our skating was far from flawless, the routines were sketchy, yet
we received enthusiastic applause for our efforts.

This was a singularly happy interlude in the routine of our
exile. Under the surface, life in Switzerland was far from carefree.
The escape from their ancestral roots had a traumatic effect on our
parents. Born and bred in a climate of romance and fierce patriotism, they felt at a loss, wondering whether they could endure the
upheaval of change. But they sustained each other and managed
to hide their anxiety from us. Father visited the embassies and
travel agents, seeking information that would help him create
a future home for us. Finally, the day arrived when he returned
to the hotel excitedly waving shipping tickets.

The Jelinek family was on its way again. To Canada, this time.
It had been our parents' hope to emigrate to the United States.
But such plans involved a longer wait for visas, and the family
cash reserves were dwindling. Besides, Canada was known to be
warm and hospitable to immigrants and we had great need of
such kindness.

Father explained carefully to us that Canada had a democratic
constitution and an added advantage—its second official language
was French. And in Switzerland, we were rapidly becoming the

Swiss (French-speaking) Family Jelinek. Later, of course, we found
out that only in Quebec do the people speak French.

Our parents made elaborate plans for the new venture. While
it was a new beginning, it was also a time of spiritual inventory.
We were leaving behind something of ourselves, the Czech heritage
which embraces a fierce love of independence with a passionate
vibrant joy in living. We were taking with us the Czech genes
that contributed to our respect for a healthy physique and the outdoor sports life.

Incidentally, we children had much to unlearn, since our growing years had coincided with both the Nazi and Communist take-
overs of our country. We were naturally expected to attend school
and the dictatorship school teachers were experts in the indoctri-
nation of their propaganda. During the Nazi regime, our older
brothers were taught to say "Heil Hitler, instead of hello, good
morning, good evening." And to make sure that our parents did
likewise. After the Reds usurped power, Richard came home from
school one day, completely bewildered. He announced that the
class has been ordered to call Father a "Bloodsucker."

"Because he's an industrialist; all industrialists are enemies of
the State," Richard sobbed.

If the brainwashing of his children weren't enough to crush
Father's spirit, there was the added burden of having his home
and factory confiscated. Added to this was the unforgettable horror
of Jan Masaryk's death and the searing memory of Lidice.

It was about Lidice that our parents spoke often in the days
before our takeoff to Canada. Frank has since said that it was as
though they were determined to leave the imprint of that horror
in our minds, so we would never forget the courage and sacrifices
of our countrymen, and perhaps one day in our own way make up
for them. We were free. But what bloody memories we were leaving behind.

chapter eight

OUR PARENTS ARE IN THE HABIT OF READING aloud to each other, and often we children were included in the listening group. One of the family's favorites, during those first months in Canada, was a section of *Romeo and Juliet* in Act III, near the beginning of Scene 3.

> They are free men, but I am banished:
> And say'st thou yet, that is not death?
> Hadst thou no poison mix'd, no sharp-ground knife.
> No sudden mean of death, though ne'er so mean,
> But 'banished' to kill me?
> 'Banished?'
> O, friar, the damned use that word in hell;
> Howling attends it; how hast thou the heart,
> Being a divine, a ghostly confessor
> A sin-absolver, and my friend profess'd
> To mangle me with that word 'banished?'

The lines had great meaning for us, particularly for Father and Mother during the first years in our adopted country. We were indeed lonely aliens in a strange land. There are, Father often explained to us, two kinds of immigrants. Many people become voluntary expatriates as they leave in search of new experiences and adventures. But for us, leaving our home was the only way to insure survival and consequently it proved indeed the most bitter exile.

89

Fortunately, the holiday spirit bound us together with comfort and balm. We assembled around the Christmas tree, as darkness fell on Christmas eve and we sang carols, particularly the carol that linked the old land with the new—that of the tenth century monarch, Good King Wenceslaus and his page. As we chanted, images of old Czech friends floated through our minds. We knew that in our homeland, living conditions were daily growing worse. Letters that occasionally eluded the Communist censors hinted at harrowing hardships and impossible working and living conditions. There was an appalling scarcity of food. Heads of families were thrown into jail, ousted executives of industry were working as laborers to feed their kin, spies filtered into the pews of Roman Catholic and Protestant Churches, party agents were planted in office and schools, neighbor spied on neighbor and children on their parents.

In a sorrowful manner, the awful news managed to bring our family closer together. With so few outside resources to turn to for amity and consolation, we clung together. As a result, the first Christmas in Canada had a depth and warmth to it far beyond that we remembered of the more affluent years.

In time, problems of adjustment gradually disappeared and friendships were established.

Fortunately, Father was not financially wiped out. We were never hungry or homeless, although there was some concern, from time to time, about meeting grocery bills or tuition fees. But whenever an emergency arose, Mother met it with poise and good humor. The family heirlooms and the beautiful collection of jewels which Father had given her gradually disappeared. Even her favorite ring, a sapphire and diamond, was exchanged for dollars. The principal reason for this dollar hunger stemmed from Father's determination to provide for us on a long range basis. The only way to accomplish this goal was to set himself up again in business. This plan involved investment in machinery, ensuring supplies of raw materials and finding buyers for the finished products. Canada was virgin territory for cork products; the problem was to convince the country that it had need of Jelinek merchandise. This proved to be a long, almost unendurable struggle.

Father had selected Oakville, a pleasant community on the shore of Lake Ontario and a few miles west of Toronto because it was central to the areas, both in Canada and the United States, where he hoped to develop the cork business.

A visitor coming to our home saw the Jelineks in action. If Mother were wretched at the separation from home and youthful roots, there was no indication of it in her serene and smiling countenance. Father, playing with his brood, maintained an equal calm; Father, of husky voice and often fierce exterior, allowing his inner gentleness to shine through as he played with us; Father, struggling so valiantly in middle age to start a new life that was hedged in with so many obstacles.

There were many plus factors to be found in our new home in Canada. Here, we discovered men were free to speak their minds.

Political freedom is most appreciated by those who have been deprived of it. To us, it was a rich blessing in the midst of troubles. Father made a point of reminding us of our good fortune when the going often got rough.

"You are free to speak and to move," he would repeat as if he were saying a rosary.

What we longed for most was acceptance. Acceptance from our new neighbors, acceptance from the community at large.

If many of our neighbors out of shyness inflicted privacy on us, our schoolmates certainly deprived us of it. We were natural butts for their humor. School, as a matter of fact, was an ordeal for all the young Jelineks. Our first fist fights were in defense of our clothes.

"Why do you dress so funny?" the local boys demanded.

The clothes which the Oakville youth found so ridiculous were no different from what we wore during our schooldays in Prague and in Switzerland. They were the Eton style flannel jackets, lacking collars and reveres, as was the fashion. But our new schoolmates saw them in a different light.

"Hasn't your father got enough money to buy you collars for your jackets?" we were repeatedly asked.

"Why do you talk so funny?" they demanded.

We spoke French, thinking that since Canada accepted both English and French as official languages, we would have no difficulty with communications. But to speak French in an English-language area was to risk downright hostility. We did our best to shrug off the taunts that often followed us across the school-grounds. "You dirty D.P.!"

We didn't mind being branded Displaced Persons. But dirty? Well, what boy isn't, once in a while?

Perhaps some day a sociologist will write a study of school taunts. If so, we have an ample source of material for him.

For even Maria, who was a friendly outgoing little soul, was a victim of prejudice. She made one true friend among her class-mates. But this youngster was quickly forbidden by her mother to associate with the little Jelinek girl, "because she's a refugee."

So while we brothers could stick together, it was harder on Maria. And more difficult still for our parents. Their ability to adjust to a new environment was put to a series of severe tests. Those first years of the 1950's were for them exercises in discipline, self control and faith. No doubt, Father spent many sleepless nights, trying to create the base for new ventures that would provide for us. Mother's quiet acceptance of hardships probably aroused anguish as well as admiration in his loving heart. Seeing her careworn face, he must have thought back to the gay, laughing Jara, who tossed her head in disdain when she suspected his ad-miration was for her mother; the beautiful carefree girl who had danced through life and motherhood until that moment in the road when a German officer informed her of the Nazis intention to take over Czechoslovakia. How much she had endured since then, and how valiantly she had withstood stress and anguish. Father was born a Catholic and although Mother is Protestant, and we were brought up in her church, his deep abiding faith in his God has never wavered. He is not one for overt prayers any-more than for obvious patriotism. But the well of feeling and integrity runs deep in him. There is no doubt in my mind that during those years, Father had many private conversations with his Lord.

We had not lived long in Oakville before an Anglican minister came to call on us. He was Canon D. Russell Smith, and although we were not of his fold, he was subsequently a frequent and wel-come visitor. Not once did he betray even the hope that we would attend his Church of the Epiphany. He came to us simply as a friend; indeed, he lived his religion and put his sermons into practical use.

As a matter of fact, some evenings the Canon could have been seen in our living room on his knees. But his hands were not folded in prayer. What he was doing was sorting out lumps of cork, separating the good, close-grained specimens from the coarser ones, and sifting the coarser bits from those altogether unusable. Also the others, including little Maria and me were his fellow helpers.

Bits of cork were strewn over the carpet, even on Mother's precious Persian rug that decorated the other end of the room. That rug was Mother's last treasure and she was holding it in reserve, in case the cork business would need another piece of machinery.

Now she thought, "We are in business again. Perhaps I needn't sell my Persian, after all."

Father suddenly found himself in a rosy optimistic mood. The future seemed assured. For here was the first cork consignment that had arrived from suppliers in Portugal and Spain, the same companies that had supplied the Prague Jelinek plant before the Communist grab. They had sent the present shipment on credit, thanks to the fair dealings that had been the family practice since our great grandfather Jelinek set up the first cork factory.

It was no wonder the Canon and the kids caught his excitement. They were all convinced they were taking part in a splendid venture, the relaunching of a once successful and prosperous establishment.

The Canon often remarked that he could get a mighty good sermon out of cork. It has buoyancy, he would say with a thoughtful smile. It refuses to sink in the sea of tribulation. It has a persistant liveliness even when it is beset by intense pressures. It wants to be allied with other materials in order to achieve supreme usefulness. It is unchanging and fits into every environment.

While the Canon pondered his sermons, Father was frantically searching for buyers for the finished corks. Many once successful European businessmen have failed to make good in the United States and Canada, and for a time it looked as though Father might be counted among them. Since nobody had ever manufactured corks in Canada until Father started his plant, he had a double difficulty. He had to float a new product before he was familiar with Canadian business methods. His suggestion that

Canada could utilize the efforts of a cork plant were met with humor and derision.

"A Canadian cork factory will never be able to compete with Portuguese and Spanish plants, where wages are about one dollar per day," Ottawa officials told him.

When you have touched bottom, there is no way to go but up. This was a philosophy that guided Father during those long dreary days when he made the rounds of government offices, hoping to persuade officials of the validity of barter deals. He approached the Departments of Trade and Commerce both in Ottawa and Washington, and in each place, they told him with finality, "No horse trading deals, please, Mr. Jelinek."

Years later they came to grasp the usefulness of Father's plan. In time, more than one European country became involved with him in such business transactions.

His concept was simple. We bought cork from Portugal and Spain. Now the Portuguese and Spaniards wanted Canadian rye and American bourbon. But they lacked the dollars to pay for them. Father's solution—a swap of cork for whisky. Not one dollar changed hands between North American liquor interests and the Portugese and Spanish cork growers. Then Father arranged another swap deal with the government of Sweden, getting for our plant the wood tops necessary for the corks. Father imported the wood tops and the Liquor Commission in Sweden used the dollars he sent in payment to buy Canadian and American liquor. The distilleries involved were Seagram, Hiram Walker and Sons and Schenley.

As a result, the cork business began to flourish. Father opened plants in Lockport, New York and in Oakville, Canada. The irony is that Father used in all these dealings the same simple barter idea that had enabled him to get from the Communists the passport that started us all on the road to Freedom.

So we began to take root in Oakville. "No one is displaced for long," Mother has said. We had lost a world, but out of our loss has come a new world, molded by pride and will and God's guidance. Pride, she has always cautioned us, doesn't mean arrogance, but simply the skill to shape bits and pieces of an old vase into a new and useful vessel.

Mother had infinite understanding, born, no doubt, of her

ordeals. She even understood when I said shamefacedly, "I hope you don't mind if I don't kiss you before my friends, Mama. But I kiss you in my mind."

That was the first step in the Americanization of Henry, Jr.

The house Father bought in Oakville had been built a century ago by missionaries as a church for the Indians. It was as solid as the oaks that shaded the lawn and it proved to be a warm, rambling nest for the Jelineks. Fine old Jacobean cabinets that our parents had brought over from England made a substantial background for the Czechoslovakian bric-a-brac that gave the rooms an air of lightness and grace. The glassed-in rear porch looked out over the turbulent waters of Lake Ontario, where in the summertime months, we learned to water ski and pilot a motor boat.

For us children, the easing of immigrant hardship meant joyful freedom again; freedom as we scarcely remembered it, freedom to be young and playful and full of mischief. But we were soon reminded of the high intent and serious purpose of the future.

In addition to his normal vitality and drive, Father now added a new component: a drive for acceptance in a new environment. It was a drive experienced early in the Twentieth Century by the emigrants who flooded the shores of the United States. Families like the Joseph Kennedys are a rich example of its ambitions and goals. The pursuit of excellence is still the primary family goal, but it is modified by simple human needs—to prove that if you cannot blend with a new culture and conform to it, at least your individuality can shape itself into a reason for admiration and acceptance.

That our difference made us individual and was responsible for our determination to shine did not lessen our need to become one of the group. We longed to have Father join the Rotarians; we were rather embarrassed to be different. Our hunger to excel first showed itself, naturally, in sports.

Frank was the first to show a promise of long range success in national sports. Since Frank branded himself as lazy, it came somewhat as a surprise to his school teachers and fellow students when he carried off first prize for almost all track and field events at his first school meet in Canada. He won the championship Victor Ludorum trophy with a points margin over the runner-up, well beyond that which Maria and Otto were able to achieve in their peak skating form. Frank was placed in eight events. One performance of his broke the school record for the 100-yard dash. Although Frank was a new student and there was some lack of school enthusiasm for his feat, it did not go unnoticed by the experts.

Richard, on the other hand, showed a singular lack of interest in outdoor sports. Whenever he accompanied Mother to the market, he never had more than one hand free for her parcels, since there was always a book tucked under the other arm. From childhood on, it was plain to all of us that Richard was the studious one. In a family noted for its dedication to sports, he remained the odd man out. A visit to the library was for him more fascinating than a view of any athletic games. Even books on sports were ignored; what interested him mostly were plans for turning wheels and intricate engines. His early promise of academic distinction was accompanied by bouts of absentmindedness that inspired us to call him The Professor even before his high school graduation. Once, when he was in his early teens, Mother took him into Oakville to buy new shoes. He was amiable; he made no criticism of her choice. Then with a vague polite smile, he wandered out of the shop.

"Richard!" Mother called after him. "Richard, come back here."

But he had taken a book out of his jacket pocket and was immersed in it. He must have made quite an odd impression on passersby as he walked down the street, reading. For he had left his new pair of shoes on the floor of the fitting room—with his old pair alongside them.

If Richard was unconcerned about his footwear, Maria and Otto made up for his disinterest. They were mad about boots; skating boots, that is. In 1950, Maria was eight and Otto ten. Those were the "bad boy" years for Otto; his mischief overflowed like a sparkling stream that flooded its banks. Yet he was so irrepressible, so full of his own zany logic that most of the time, the family forgave him his misdeeds. Otto, unlike myself, was never ashamed to show his affection for Mother. When he was small, he would come and sit beside her, put his head in her lap, the wild energy momentarily stilled. On skates, he was a loyal partner to

Maria. He was already a fiend for practice and Maria's interest in the less important phases of the sport—such as a change from brown leather lace-up boots to the more elegant white buckskins —bored him. At this period, ten-year-old Otto just took off on the ice for sheer physical joy. His days of fastidious attention to every detail of the art were far in the future.

I brought up the rearguard as the compliant fellow traveler. I ran with Frank, listened to Richard, played truant with Otto and long remained secretly jealous of Maria's skill on ice.

Father was staunchly at the helm, guiding us with a firm discipline. Each of us was hauled before him, if not for mutiny at least for misdeeds. Every trial saw Mother in the role of defense attorney. Even as we tried to outfox Father, we couldn't help but respect his acumen. We never got the best of him, which is true even to this day.

Although our family is sports-oriented, we have inherited from our parents a sense of objectiveness that makes us somewhat ironic in self-appraisal. In writing about himself in relation to the family, Frank has made some pointed self criticism.

"When the Jelinek family emigrated to Canada in 1948," Frank writes, "Frank was at this time a constant source of concern to his parents. The elder Jelineks had to start a new life in a strange country with five children to support and hardly any money left or friends to help them. Even so, the children were sent to private schools, while the parents worked long and hard.

"Frank went to school in Canada for only two years before he graduated. Then he joined his father's cork business."

Thus Frank dismisses blithely the financial stresses of those years. The truth is that he might have achieved a combination of academic distinction and practical acumen had circumstances been different. He was, at eighteen, literally sharing the family burden. After high school graduation, he carried bags of cork, earning a laborer's pay. It had been his secret dream to embark on the study of medicine. But he was all too conscious of Father's business struggles.

"You've had troubles enough," he told Father. "I'm going to help." He jettisoned his personal ambitions and switched his attention to the business.

At that time, Frank had the smooth baby face that would, he feared, jeopardize his acceptance as a businessman.

"Frank, my boy, why don't you grow a mustache?" Father suggestedly grandly. "It would suit you and certainly help in your job as foreman of fifty odd girls, some of them very attractive."

Frank snorted; the idea didn't appeal to him at all. Whereupon Father made a deal with him. He would give his son a dollar per day for each day Frank refrained from shaving his upper lip. Our brother, who was always in need of money, accepted. He had a pretty good thing going for him until one day, Father abrogated the contract. The mustache was now an independent growth, and besides Frank had demonstrated that youth was no handicap to supervising and selling. But Frank clung to the hairy ornament on his upper lip. It has become a merit badge of commerce.

How does one write about Otto?

Otto is Pan on skates. He rules by charm and breaks all rules. He has inherited his share of the shortcomings that characterize the rest of the Jelinek males. He is stubborn, easily upset, visibly nervous, somewhat dictatorial and in some instances rather lazy. When it came to our studies, Father was hard to please. Richard and I, young as I was, worried about our marks. Fifty is the passing grade in Canada, but naturally we whipped our minds into producing much higher results in order to satisfy Father.

Whenever report card time rolled around, poor Richard was a nervous wreck. Not so with Otto. He carried himself with an air of insouciance that convinced us that for once, he had outdone himself. We all gathered in a circle around Father, who was awaiting the reports.

"Richard," he said.

"Eighty," Richard answered, cowering.

"Eighty?" Father asked. "Why not ninety? And you, Otto?"

Otto looked positively triumphant. "I did well, Father. I knew my studies."

"The marks, Otto."

"Fifty-one."

Richard's eighty was expected of him: Otto's passing plus one was a cause for rejoicing. At dinner that night, the family toasted him.

"How well you did, Otto. Fifty-one. Think of that."

Mischief-making was practically a full time occupation with Otto. The energies that were later to make him the superb skater were directed in oddball outlets. The house in Oakville, like the fine old stone mansion in Prague, was ideal for a growing boy who had to test the stretches of his imagination. The attic of the old mansion was an invitation to anyone young at heart. Here Otto built a fort of empty cork bags and furnished it with blankets and provisions. But he had the foresight to acquire two homes long before such ownership became a status symbol. He created a tree house high in a maple. His talent for scrounging showed itself magnificently that autumn, for somehow he was always amply supplied with funds for bus fares and movie admissions. And I must say he was generous with me, the willing follower.

"School's a bore," Otto decided. "You can learn more watching nature. Agreed, Henry?"

"Agreed," I said with all the fervor of an adoring kid brother.

Watching nature, a procedure that included sitting in the tree house, pretending to be pioneer scouts or napping in the fort, didn't teach us much about flora and fauna, but we certainly were indoctrinated in the fine points of truancy.

We began the day with a circumspect breakfast to throw Mother off the track. Mother was delighted with our voracious appetites. Life on the shore of Lake Ontario agreed with her young sons, she decided, plying us with an extra rasher of bacon or hot sweet rolls.

"Their appetites are improving," she said fondly to Father.

What Mother didn't realize is that the trencherman's breakfast had to sustain us until the evening meal. Usually we had lunch at school, but since we had taken our own leave of that institution, there wasn't much chance of foraging a hearty midday meal.

However, after the first week, Otto's talent for improvisation improved mightily. He contrived to lift a tin of tomato juice, a chunk of bread, a piece of fruit and secrete it about his person. During the morning, we used to watch Mother from our vantage point in the tree house and when she left for a trip to the market, Otto shinnied down the trunk and Indian fashion skulked into the kitchen. He was careful never to grab too much at one time.

"I can't understand it," Mother said at dinner one night, "I was sure I laid in a supply of tomato juice, but there is only one tin in the cupboard."

We had lunch either in the tree house, at the bottom of the garden sloping to the shore, or in our fort, wherever we happened to be. We rigged up a sun clock at the foot of the maple in order to keep a rough tab on time. The fort was naturally more comfortable, but there was the hazard of creeping into the house. The old mission stairs had an audible creak and Father has unusually sensitive ears. One afternoon, while we were on bivouac in the fort, there was the sound of footsteps outside the attic. We scurried trembling under the cork sacks. But the steps paused at the entrance of the attic. It was Father, and he was making one of his casual tours of the house.

Another time, when Otto decided we should be rewarded with a trip to the movies, he had just enough money for admission. So, getting to town was the problem. He decided therefore that we would ignore the city bus, which demanded fares and risk taking the children's school bus. We had to duck in our seats as the bus drove past the school gates and the rest of the poor little inmates descended. Otto made the ducking realistic—he dropped his pen at that point in our journey. If you wonder what he was doing with a pen, why he was making up our report cards naturally.

Otto never made the error of marking himself too high. He was more generous with me.

"Henry seems to be doing well this semester," Mother told Father. "I am so pleased."

"Mother," Frank said casually one afternoon, "How are the boys?"

"They are well," Mother said.

"Is that so? Well, which one has the temperature?"

"Neither," Mother said, and then a worried expression crept over her face. I was in the kitchen, pilfering a sweet before dinner, and hearing Frank's questions, I knew the game was up. I tried to make myself inconspicuous, but Frank caught me by the arm, "Where are you going?" he asked. "Wait, I have something to ask you. Tell me, how is Otto's serious illness?"

I tried my best to look like the Good Soldier Schweik, but Mother panicked instantly. "What do you mean, Otto's illness? Do you know something you are keeping from me?"

"I met one of Otto's teachers this afternoon," Frank said, "and he commiserated with me. He thought it must be difficult for you, Mother, to have to attend two sick boys for three weeks."

That Otto is a worrier is indicated by his occasional inability to sleep at night. That he is not always completely reliable is shown by his lack of planning; by his less than cavalier attitude toward the girls who adore him; by forgetting family birthdays and usually being overdrawn at the bank. He often changes his mind about his future goals; he is vacillating about investments and usually delays making a decision until the moment of crisis. Usually he is generous, but once in a while he grows painfully frugal, and then whenever he telephones our parents, he reverses the toll charge.

As he matured, Otto showed a happy tendency to calm down. His family would be the first to agree on his fine qualities, which include absolute loyalty and devotion to the clan, a sense of humor, a talent for communicating with the world, his commendable thrift (when it doesn't go to extremes), his pride in himself and his work.

His father has a habit of referring to him as "that bum." But this is only camouflage for the absolute admiration and unflagging love for him.

The pain of adjustment to a new country, new habits, new friends was lessening. The family was now firmly entrenched into the Oakville environment. We were comfortable. Our new neighbors had finally begun to understand us and we to understand them. Father and Mother were at ease; the business was flourishing; the children were growing. Whatever trauma had been a handicap to us in the beginning of our Canadian life was gradually dissolving. But it was not characteristic of us Jelineks to glide along. The ice was firm enough now to serve as a foundation for new and outgoing ambitions. As Frank said, the moment the ground was solid under us, we courted new challenges. Perhaps the years of stress had conditioned us to stretch our beings to the fullest.

Anyway, suddenly it was the time of the Red Robins.

chapter nine

I<small>T WAS THE WINTER OF 1952; THE WINDS WERE</small> cruel and piercing, the waves roared in from the lakefront and over the radio, you heard a gay old lively tune, "When the red, red robin comes a-bob, bob, bobbin' along."

Canada is a dream country for skaters. The smooth glitter of ice dots the landscape; frozen ponds, narrow rivers, man-made rinks coax the skills of the human frame.

That winter's evening Mother sat in the tiers of an ice arena. She was snugly wrapped in furs, but the stirring of her blood was enough to keep her warm. For she was about to witness the Canadian debut of her son and daughter in an ice show and when a dream is ripe to blossom into reality, the north winds have the effect of Florida zephyrs.

Suddenly, the spotlight pinned them to the diamond sparkle of the ice, her young ones—Otto in crimson tights that hugged his wiry preadolescent frame too snugly, Maria in red, too, with an absurd tuft of feathers on her round little bottom. They blinked. The lights blinded them, keeping them from spotting Mother. Which was just as well, as unsteady of gait, they careened across the ice in the first routine they had ever attempted.

Mother sat upright, clutching the hand of the woman beside her. Mother suffered and prayed as Otto and Maria finished their routine to generous applause, evidently more for their courage than their skill.

"They are yours?" the woman beside Mother asked sympathetically.

Mother nodded, and embarrassed, withdrew her hand. Then she hurried out to supervise the little birds' exit. There was within her heart a tremulous feeling of elation mixed with fear. Her dream was taking substance, and she wondered uneasily what the future had in store for her little red robins.

There was a gentle hollow in our front lawn, which eventually became the core of the swimming pool. But in those days, we simply sprayed it with a hose each frosty night and thus created our own rink. Here you would find Otto and Maria every day after school, practicing loops and gliding lines. With growing confidence in their technique, they examined their traces with the wisdom of embryo experts. An hour of practice in the biting cold; two hours; three. Then Maria, crying plaintively, "I'm going in, Otto."

Otto: "No, wait a bit."

"But I'm freezing."

Otto, as dominant with Maria as he'd been with me during our hooky period, orders: "Let's get going again with the sit-spin. We must learn to keep our backs straight. Remember how the coach back home—I mean, in Prague—used to stress it?"

Maria, wavering, pauses to watch Otto sit and spin.

"Don't let yourself wobble," she cautions him. "You're not doing it right."

Otto comes out of a spin and draws himself up to his full length. "What do you mean, 'Not doing it right'? I kept my back straight—"

"You did not! You were bending over so much you were sticking out—"

From the house, Mother calls, "Maria! Otto! Supper."

Off with the skates; an end to the spins and winter chills for the night.

If the life of the immigrant is hard, it is no more difficult in its relation to reality than the life of the skater. In both instances, the demands, the sacrifices, the discipline are larger than life. Faith plays a strong role, too, and faith is an ingredient that was part of the Jelinek tradition. During this period, Otto's rebellion simmered down and abruptly took a new dynamic direction. And Maria no longer wept to her dolls in the dark night, the old painful litany, "I want to go home."

There are two sides to the life of a skater. Spectators in comfortable rink-side seats take vicarious delight in the sight of the lovely girls and wiry lads swooping and skimming over the ice. It is indeed an entrancing sight; all the seemingly effortless leaps and lifts, turns and twists, the soaring beauty that seems to defy the laws of gravity. There is glamor in the winning of gold medals and silver trophies. There is satisfaction in the applause that marks peak achievements, the spins and pirouettes, the fantastic precision of dreamy routines that equal for fantasy and charm the prewar waltzes of old Vienna.

But behind the glamor of public appearance, there is the lonely discipline of the dedicated craftsman. Miles of practice; hundreds of hours on skates, all executed before an audience of one—the coach, whose blame is inevitably more frequent than his praise. To please the coach is the ambition of every pupil, but a grudgingly kind word comes only when you have achieved near perfection.

Imagine a morning in the Jelinek household in Oakville. It is now five A.M. Over Lake Ontario, the silver moon pierces the dark. The sun is still hiding. The house groans and creaks like an old man with arthritic bones as the heat comes through the steam pipes. The small travelling clock on the night table beside our parents' bed shrills its alarm. A hand reaches out to smother the sound. Not all of the menage is to be so rudely jarred out of tranquil sleep. Only Mother and the two whom she has designated as the future skating champions of the world.

Mother pads softly into Otto's room. The dim night-light reveals only a mound of untidy bedclothes. Somewhere under this heap, Otto is buried in sound sleep.

"Time," Mother says softly.

Otto usually needs but one summons. But the night is cold, and he is an unsound sleeper to whom rest comes with difficulty. He has not yet had sufficient measure of sleep for a healthy energetic lad.

"What?" he asks with a grunt. "What?"

But already he has spun around on the bed to complete the

hurricane results of his bedding. He recognizes Mother and demands plaintively, "Why can't I sleep a bit longer?"

"You can sleep on, if you want to." Mother knows how to handle her son. "We'll forget about skating today."

Skating is the magic word. He is suddenly wide awake, eager for what the session will bring, the outer edge, inner edge, figure eights, turns, twists, spins and jumps. Yes, he is alert, dark eyes sparkling, smile wide and ingratiating, body springy as a Jack-in-the-box. He is full of optimism; it will be a good day, successful, with no danger of knee-cracking, head-splitting tumbles.

In the room across the hall, filled with the memorabilia of Maria's childhood, dolls and stuffed animals, Mother's only daughter is deep in a sweet child's sleep. Maria's boyish looks have blossomed into a dimpled beauty. Her dark thick hair is spread over the pillow, the only touch of disorder in a bed still as neat as it was at bedtime. A somewhat prim Sleeping Beauty, Mother thinks, as she repeats the morning summons. With Maria, it is always less of a chore. There is no suggestion of a whirlwind here. Maria opens her wide brown eyes at once and rewards Mother with a bright smile. Mother trips down to the kitchen, certain that by the time she has prepared breakfast, Maria will have donned her skating costume.

She couldn't be more wrong. Maria's intentions are good, but her healthy young body craves more rest. Her face wreathed in a beatific smile, she drifts off into a pleasant slumber. Shortly, it is necessary for Mother to repeat the routine.

Maria is alert and bright, but she does have a lamentable talent for taking a nap at inopportune moments. She has fallen asleep on the ice—twice, in fact. The first episode took place in an ice carnival in Oakville. Maria was cast in the role of Sleeping Beauty; Otto was Prince Charming. The opening scene found Maria lying on a snow bed, bathed in soft lights and dreamy music. Otto planted a kiss on his sister's cheek, the signal that she was to awake from her deep sleep. Nothing happened; Maria was far away, her dreams accented by a delicate little snore. Otto glanced at the orchestra, hoping it would repeat several bars. But the music followed in sequence, so with a frantic turn of skates, he began to improvise. Sailing around the bed, he repeated the kiss, adding this time, "Maria, get moving. Wake up!"

Was it a pinch, together with that brotherly kiss, that finally achieved results? The two differ in their version. But the Princess did awaken. She skated exquisitely and charmed everyone.

Except Otto. He never minces words when he is angry with our sister.

"What got into you?" he demanded. "You let us down."

What he didn't realize was that the problem was quite elemental. Maria was an early-to-bed girl. Nine o'clock was her deadline. To perform beyond that hour was always an ordeal for her, but when the hour stretched to eleven and beyond, she could scarcely control her reflexes. She was literally asleep on her feet.

Even Otto admits somewhat grudgingly that his partner is usually dependable. But this did happen once more. At that time, toward midnight, Maria was skating solo in a dance test. Suddenly the judges and spectators realized something was amiss. Her silver skates slowed down until finally they reached a complete halt. There she stood in the center of the arena, quite alone, utterly exquisite, her long legs that had so recently flashed in a lovely waltz rhythm quite still, her torso in its brief skating skirt a statuesque support for her sleepy little head.

"Maria, Maria—"

The shout came from the judges' box and pierced the sleepy head. Maria awakened, startled, suddenly conscious of her fluff. She pushed off to skate, achieving pace to blend with the music and the movements of the dance. But it was too late. Her score marks had dwindled. It was long before Otto forgave her, since her lapse had badly jeopardized his own chances of passing and Otto is very concerned with his pursuit of excellence. Nevertheless, he is also extremely solicitous of our sister. These two have always been close. When Maria, as an infant, was put in her playpen, Otto, two and a half years her senior, was put in the "cage" with her. He has always looked after her.

The voice that had tried to jar Maria into waking was that of their coach, Bruce Hyland.

Bruce has become by osmosis, part of the Jelinek family. He often arrived at the house at five in the morning to breakfast with Otto and Maria. Perhaps he felt the contrast between the warm cozy kitchen and the bleak ice rink would be less painful to take if he accompanied his fledglings from their nest.

Maria and Otto (1961).   Maria and Otto (1963).

At the Olympic Games, Squaw Valley (1960).

Mr. and Mrs. Jelinek watch Maria and Otto skate at Davos, Switzerland (1961).

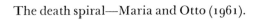

The death spiral—Maria and Otto (1961).

Maria, Otto and Henry, Jr.—playing it for laughs (1961).

Maria, Otto, Coach Bruce Hyland and some of their Canadian team mates depart for Prague (1961).

Elegance on ice.

Unless you have seen it, you will find it impossible to imagine the condition of a skating arena at dawn. There are no spotlights, no band, no tinsel, no silver skates. It is grim, cheerless and empty with only the distant hum of a generator breaking the bleak silence. The benches, row on row of them, are deserted, peopled only with the ghosts of previous carnivals.

Bruce laces his own skates with the speed of a professional.

"Ready, kids?" he asks.

"Come on, Maria," Otto says brusquely. "You're always so slow."

"I can't help it. My bootlace broke."

"You should have seen to it before."

"Easy, kids." Bruce is always the mediator. "We've got work to do. Let's not argue."

In the chilly arena, Bruce and Otto set up the record player and put on the records they had brought with them. Music, Maestro! Maria links hands with Otto and off they go, skimming around the rink in a warm-up exercise. Maria's pigtails flatten out as they speed along.

"Okay, kids," Bruce says. "Now to work."

Now that exercise has defrosted their frozen bodies, they are no longer envious of his heavy mitts, padded parka and the hidden red longjohns that are his habitual secret weapon against the bitter cold.

"Let's do the slow bits first," he suggests. "You have to feel the music in this section. Don't be too slow. Try it, while I count to the music."

He places the needle half way between the center of the disc and its edge; he has done this often, starting the melody at the bar he wants, so now he can pinpoint the needle every time, almost without looking. Otto and Maria satisfy him for a few minutes, then he halts them. "Stop!" he shouts, his breath steaming above the ice. "You kept too far apart. This is a pair, remember? Not a couple of solos."

"It was Maria," Otto blurts out. "She went out too far."

Maria, with an imperious toss of pigtails, denies the accusation. "I didn't, you big—"

"Let's begin again," Bruce says, cutting her short, in mid-sentence. His calm professional manner curbs their temperaments.

They repeat their routine. They are working hard, as the flood of perspiration testifies. Hoping for a kind word from their coach, they skid-stop eager and supplicating before him. "No, no, no," he says, stopping the record and going into minute post-mortem of all their errors.

They listen. Again they flash across the ice. Again and again. They come in time to enjoy it. For no skater ever reaches the top without first having to learn to love the sport with a deep and abiding love that discounts the endless practice. All the sweat, the numbing cold, Bruce's everlasting, "Just once more, kids," is part of the price the sport exacts from its devoted disciples.

What makes a satisfactory practice session? Otto's assessment is this: A workout is good if during its time span he has been able to hoist Maria in the air fifty times without a hitch.

Incidentally, Maria's weight is a delicate problem in our house. Not that she's heavy, but Otto watches her every mouthful. In a restaurant, he will lift her plate, to see how much more he will have to lift when they are skating. For several years they had a ballet master to help them with their stretching exercises. He was teaching Otto lifts and as Maria jumped into his arms, the delicate fellow crumpled to the ice with two fractured ribs. Unfortunately, he weighed 125 and Maria weighed 140. Since then, she has thinned down considerably.

Otto has a voracious appetite for steaks and roast beef; he's addicted to German dishes, particularly sauerbraten, but the exasperating thing is that he never puts on an ounce. Whenever Mother looks at him with envy, he reminds her that he has been skating an average of two hours each day, 365 days in each year. "With a day off every leap year," he adds with his Otto grin.

Nothing irks him more than to hear some football hero dismiss skating as a sissy sport.

In their years of preparation, a hard day at school usually followed the early morning practice sessions. Often, Bruce met them after class for another training period. Maria learned how to wriggle out of her school frock and shrug into her skating skirt in the back of the car as she was driven to the rink. Truck drivers often goggled whenever a traffic light forced them to halt alongside this mobile dressing room. Maria affected not to notice them. Of course, in our Prague days, it had been easier: the limousine was larger and Maria was smaller.

Hooky from school to practice on ice was forbidden. Father was adamant on that point. "Failure in any one of the subjects for either of you and all skating stops," he announced. Fortunately, Otto managed to skim by most of the time with his glorious 51 marks. Maria, as usual, was a joy to the family. She had a natural aptitude for languages, particularly French and she adored mathematics and history. What she liked most about the venerable Romans were their baths. After icy sessions on the practice rink, she dreamed of steamy Roman baths scented with rare perfumes. Nevertheless, the cold never had a deleterious effect on her. Her skin glowed like pink satin. Even when her hands grew icy, she refused to wear gloves. It was necessary to have a safe grip on Otto's hands as she soared over his head in one of their magnificent lifts. As a result her fingers took long to thaw out.

At school, the first class was often over before she could hold her pen properly.

However, when she and Otto skip a practice session, their muscles stiffen and the aftermath isn't worth the indulgence. It takes too many warming up exercises to restore to the body its supple strength. They both shake their arms and legs. Otto walks around on his hands before each performance, a trick that arouses awe from the stage crew. As a rule, many skaters have found that it is simpler to stick to discipline, and that discipline had strengthened not only muscles but character.

One morning, while Bruce was waiting for the kids to get into their skating costumes, he sat in the warm kitchen drinking coffee.

"Mrs. Jelinek," he announced, "I think Maria and Otto should go to Ottawa next week for the skating competition."

"Oh, no!" Mother was flustered. "They're still much too young."

"Do you, or do you not, want to make world champions of them?" Bruce's voice was calm but there was an amused gleam in his shrewd eyes. For only two years ago, at their first meeting, Mother had put to him a similar question. "Can you make world champions out of them?" she had asked. This happened shortly after she heard Bruce had been appointed instructor in the local Figure Skating Club. She had invited him for dinner and later arranged for him to work with Maria and Otto. That night, Bruce had answered wisely, "It is still too early to say. But I shall try."

And now, Mother was faced with her original wish. "Why, yes . . . of course," she said. "But I'm not sure they will do well in Ottawa. And it would be such a pity if they became discouraged."

"Well, at least, we'll be able to see how they stand up in competition," Bruce suggested.

Mother reluctantly agreed. After all, Bruce knew what was best for them. So off they went the following week to the Canadian capital. The trial was a surprising success. Otto and Maria were placed a third. Thus they were launched on the road to competitive skating.

chapter ten

ALTHOUGH OUR PARENTS WERE ABSORBED IN THE promising career of the young skaters, they did not neglect the rest of us. Indeed, the warmth of the family hearth gave us all the strength and courage to test our wings.

If Frank was Father's surrogate, Richard was Mother's helper. Perhaps Richard, who is more sensitive than the rest of the Jelinek men, appreciated the weight of Mother's responsibilities and did his best to lighten them. Whenever our parents had an engagement in the evening, Richard cared for us younger ones. He would dump all three of us—Otto, Maria and myself—in the tub and scrub us until our cheeks and ears were flaming red. Then he would announce to Mother, who was dressing for the evening, "Mother, the children are in bed and all right." It sounded very touching to her, since he was only a boy himself.

We all look back on those years with affection and nostalgia. Mother's young brother, Denis, had escaped from Czechoslovakia and had come to Canada with us. He worked in Toronto and spent his weekends with us. He had been in his last year of college when he fled Prague, and he was just ten years older than our brother Frank. He spelled Richard as our babysitter. I must say that we gave him a hard time. Imagine having four energetic nephews and a niece gang up on you. He was tall and lean and our favorite name for him was Spaghetti, which didn't endear us to him. Nevertheless, he was as devoted to us as Nana, the shaggy governess in Peter Pan, and he was forever chasing after us with frustrating results. Whenever we pelted him with snowballs, the barrage would infuriate him so much that in his anger, he'd try, like Samson, to lift a corner of the house. Often we watched television programs that he considered too violent for our young savage tastes; he would turn off the set, which was usually a signal for concerted protest on our part. Words were poor weapons; we believed in action. Four of us would pick up Denis, like some supine Greek warrior, lift him over our heads, march him out of the room, toss him on a sofa, brush off our hands, return to the playroom and lock the door against his fury. He invariably blamed Frank for our misdeeds.

In more peaceful moments, Denis taught us Scrabble as an instrument for perfecting our English. The trouble was that we played for money, and in the excitement of battle, we forgot our English and lapsed into our comfortable mother tongue, so we lost out both on English and cash. Our wily uncle was a superb Scrabble player.

Denis found it difficult to adjust to his new environment. He was disturbed by the fact that we were called Slavs and to some of our Canadian neighbors this meant slaves. He lived with us for six years, and finally in 1955, he journeyed to Vienna, graduated from the University and eventually found employment there.

It is Otto's destiny to be blamed for everything that goes wrong. The truth is that he's been a culprit so often that blaming him is inevitable. For instance, when he was sent to Davos in Switzerland to a private school, the Swiss Alpine College, he was admonished to behave himself. He did, according to his own standards. He shared quarters with a boy who was a sleepwalker. Their room was directly above the girls' dormitory, and being resourceful young men, they devised a method of viewing the lovely nymphs. They would tie the sheets to the bedposts, slide down in their pajamas just far enough so they could peer into the girls' windows. Fortunately, none of the victims happened to look out of their windows; they were too busy stripping for sleep. One night, Otto's roommate landed out of the window into a snowpile. When the excitement subsided, Otto was summoned into the headmaster's office and accused of tossing his partner out head first. Otto defended himself vigorously. He explained that no doubt his roommate went to bed with visions of the goodies on the floor below, and being a sleepwalker had attempted a rehearsal for the Rape of the Sabines, an act frustrated by a torn rope sheet.

Nevertheless, Otto was punished. He was always being punished. With rare logic, the headmaster decided that if Otto were punished for something he didn't do, it would compensate for other misdeeds that he had no doubt perpetrated and of which the school was still ignorant.

Last year, Mother found in one of Frank's notebooks a contemporary character sketch of me; at least, that's what he called it. To quote from it would perhaps show my place in the life and times of the Jelinek children.

"Since he is the youngest of the five Jelinek offspring," Frank wrote with admirable self control, "Henry is still regarded as the baby of the family and is treated as such. He is the only one who, when broke, dares to touch the family for a loan. Father's stern dictum that we must all learn to live within our allowances doesn't seem to apply to Henry, Jr. He gets a handout from his doting brothers whenever he is in need. Which is often.

"He also borrows cars from his father and brothers, all of whom are rather skeptical of his ability as a racer. Within two months, he had three accidents in three separate cars plus a serious motorboat accident. These 'errors in judgment' as he calls them have cost him most of the money he earned during the year he spent out of school. Nevertheless, he had sufficient funds to treat himself to a trip through Europe, where he was greatly impressed by the time he spent in a nudist colony in Denmark.

"Like all the Jelinek boys, Henry showed a precocious interest in girls. There have been rumors that he is sometimes the gallant knight, rescuing a damsel in distress. But since the jousting place is usually a bar and the black knight the demoiselle's boy friend, Henry often bears the marks of a bruised gladiator on his body.

"As a baby, he was eager to be a man. He hated his long blond curls and got into a tantrum when he was mistaken for a girl. At five, he took a garden shears to the curls and after that pronounced himself a man, although he looked as if an Indian had recently scalped him. He was, as a boy, a poor loser, and he was known to throw darts at his opponents when he lost a game.

"He was also inclined to be lazy. When Father assigned him work in the garden, Henry took the time to perfect his golf stroke. As a skater, he enjoyed performing with Otto and Maria and liked nothing better than to upstage them. He might have developed into a skillful skater, except that he loathed practice and enjoyed only a performance before an audience. He wanted to be first or nothing.

"These characteristics are improving. He has always been generous hearted, and now that his sense of sportsmanship has improved, he is also liked by everyone. To the delight of the family he has begun to work harder at his studies, dress better, drive slower and also begins to concede that life is more than a series of parties, fast cars, pretty girls and a nudist colony."

If my eldest brother's evaluation of me stung, I had merely to read what he thought of our brother, Richard, and I was consoled.

"Richard—" so ran Frank's notes, "is unlike the other brothers in several ways. He is slim, whereas the rest of us have a tendency toward a generous girth. He has an eagle-beak, while the other Jelineks, including Maria, have been endowed with flat noses and rather sturdy necks. Richard wears glasses permanently. Although he cannot spell properly, he is the only scholar in the family.

"Whereas all other Jelineks develop a feeling of loneliness and melancholy when left alone, Richard seems to thrive on his own company. Unlike the rest of us, he does not approach sports with near fanaticism. However, he has always been extremely agile with his fingers. When he was five and I, Frank, nine, Richard easily beat me in all games involving skill of hands and fingers. It is a poorly kept secret that he was an ugly baby when he was born; it's a matter of individual opinion how much he has since improved.

"Richard is stubborn and argumentative. His teachers complain that he interrupts class to express his thoughts in a clear penetrating voice. Punishment for these outbursts never seems to discourage him.

"As if to prove to the family that he is not a maverick, Richard has participated in sports. He is a good skier, a fine long distance runner and in his junior year at high school, he was selected for the All Star Soccer Team."

Thus the saga of the Jelineks continued. But at that point the embryo skating stars took the spotlight again.

The summer after my brother and sister had had their first taste of competition, Mother took us all to Lake Placid. Our parents knew that this resort, in the Adirondacks, was the home of the great Gustav Lussi, former coach of Dick Button, who was seven times world champion and twice Olympic winner. Lussi is famous among figure skaters for his skill in teaching the fine points of jumps and spins. Otto and Maria were eager to study with him, for already in those early days, they planned to enter the Canadian Junior Pairs Championships, which were to be held the coming winter.

After Lussi took them on as pupils we had many family conclaves to weigh their chances. At that time, Lussi was trying to eradicate several of their personal idiosyncrasies. Maria, for example, had the lamentable habit of sticking out her tongue while skating. Trainer Lussi offered her a dollar reward if she could get through an entire practice session with her tongue where it rightfully belonged.

"Spectators will get the idea you're just a cheeky brat," he said.

His admonitions were in vain. Maria didn't break the habit until she took a nasty spill and bit her tongue.

Otto, meanwhile, played a double role. By day he was the hardworking young skater; by night, he was the rogue of Lake Placid. Most of the young figure skaters who took their future seriously were in bed and asleep by nine o'clock. Otto was a night bird. Waiting patiently until the last sounds ceased in the house, he would make a rope out of his bedsheets—an art at which he was already skilled—let himself down from the second floor and roar off to the movies.

Father's barter method reduced to a juvenile scale enabled Otto to accumulate funds for his escapades. Each day, during Mother's absence, he visited the refrigerator, which was always stocked with juicy oranges. He would help himself to several and then, strolling along the beach, he would offer them to vacationers at much less than Mother paid for them. This exercise in commerce continued for a good part of our vacation; only when the sheets were old one night and ripped, with a resulting fall for our young Tarzan, were Otto's exploits uncovered.

Otto had a mischievous weakness for fruit. Once before he had been involved, with what we call his "adventure with the sacred apples." Of a rare specimen, they were Father's favorites, and he was growing them experimentally in a special orchard. We were all specifically forbidden to pick fruit from these trees. One morning, we were jolted out of our beds by Father's bellow of rage. The apples were still hanging on the trees, but each apple had missing at least one bite of its succulent flesh.

"Otto!" Father thundered. "Come here, Otto!"

Whenever there was any indication of mischief, Otto was automatically summoned. Father led him out to the garden to the ravished dwarf apple trees. Otto maintained staunchly that he had abided by Father's rules. Not one juicy apple had been picked. He had simply climbed the branches, nibbled from each piece of fruit and left the core intact, still clinging by its stem to the tree. Otto always had his own code of obedience.

Three years after the first lesson with Gustav Lussi, Otto and Maria were chosen as King and Queen of Winter at Lake Placid. Stars of the calibre of Perry Como, Jo Stafford and Kirk Douglas participated in the ceremonies. The glossy coronation program was unusually kind to my brother and sister.

The Coronation Ceremony is the official inaugural event of the Lake Placid winter season. For Maria and Otto it meant recognition for their achievements in figure skating competitions, including, to that date, the Junior Canadian Pairs Championships, and the runner-up spot in the previous year's North American title competition. In their first try for world championship honors, they had already been placed third.

Their first major contest, as it happened, was one of their easiest wins.

It was the Canadian Junior Pairs Competition for which they practiced diligently under Bruce's supervision, after they got home from that first trip to Lake Placid. The night before the competition, Maria confided in Bruce that she felt they had a chance of placing second.

"Yes, you have a good chance," Bruce conceded drily. "There are only two sets of competitors anyway."

The other skating pair was lean and lanky. During the warm up period, it was evident to all present that Otto and Maria had an excellent chance of beating them. Just before the first couple was scheduled to go on, the boy began to limp. He had injured his foot.

"You certainly have a good chance of winning now," said Bruce to Maria, "since you are the only skaters competing."

My brother and sister duly performed before the judges and piled up enough points to give them title ranking. For although they were unopposed, it was still necessary for them to reach a certain standard in order to merit first place.

This is what a local newspaper wrote of the event:

"Recently, Oakville has scored a straight hit in the field of art and beauty. And the two people who have brought Oakville's name into national prominence are of the early ages of fourteen and twelve! They are Otto and Maria Jelinek, who, representing Oakville Figure Skating Club at the Canadian Figure Skating Championships held in Toronto last week, became Junior Pairs Champions.

"Not only is the Jelineks' skating of high technical exactitude and brilliance, but on the ice they make a fascinating picture with their unaffected youthfulness. Otto is a most engaging boy, bright-faced and alert in body. His sister, Maria, skating with her pigtails merry-go-rounding gaily in her self created breeze, is a vision right out of fairy-tale books.

"The Jelineks' triumph has been achieved by natural aptitude fortified by the most gruelling kind of work."

With this achievement accomplished, Otto and Maria were invited to compete in the next world championships, scheduled for the same month in Vienna. They refused the invitation and Father explained the reason to the press.

"They have trained for a three and a half minute routine for the junior competition," he said. "All senior competitions are made up of five minute routines. They simply would not have time in two weeks to whip up a longer program."

Although he made no mention of it, there was another reason for their staying away from Vienna. Politics and figure skating made dangerous bedfellows. Vienna was under the rule of four power Allied government. However, in their own zone in Austria, the Russians had absolute say, no matter what requests might be made by the British, French or Americans. Therefore, there was a definite risk in exposing the two skaters to possible political complications.

It was difficult indeed for Otto and Maria to turn down the dazzling invitation. But safety demanded it.

Mother was always in the audience when Otto and Maria performed. Seldom, in those years, was she away from them. However, at Squaw Valley in 1960, she found that the Olympic rules were separating her from her children. She was blockaded by a high fence around the Olympic "Village," where only competitors were allowed to enter.

The years under dictatorships and later in exile have made Mother adroit and resourceful. Still, her persuasive powers made no dent on the guards. So she tried to hoist herself over the fence, and being athletic, she accomplished her mission, with the result that a guard chased her right into Otto and Maria's quarters, much to their mixed horror and amusement. Later by reconnoitering, she discovered that at certain times there was only one guard at a gate, and he was under orders never to desert his post. So his chase after intruders was brief and half-hearted. But for years we used to chuckle over the memory of Mother, usually so composed and elegant, hightailing it past the sentry.

Trainer Bruce Hyland devised his own means to gain entry. He drove past the Japanese ski team and graciously offered them a lift. Then as the sentry peered into the car, Bruce said blandly, "Me Japanese chauffeur." And the sentry waved them on.

At the Squaw Valley rink, Maria and Otto were in top form. Yet when the judges put up their marks, both the young skaters and the spectators were shocked to discover they had placed fourth.

A few days later, at the World Championships at Vancouver, Otto and Maria skated less perfectly and yet were placed second. The same competitors and most of the same judges.

In the words of Dick Button, "For some unknown reason the Jelineks' marks were far below what they should have been, in view of the excellence of their performance."

Otto felt this was the greatest disappointment in his life.

But my brother and sister were by now indoctrinated in the spirit of sports competition. You accept defeat, disappointment, perhaps injustice, and the next morning you are out on skates in the rink, the past behind you and the promise of the future ahead.

Our parents had taught us well.

chapter eleven

"I T IS UNTHINKABLE," FATHER SAID, HIS VOICE strained, "You are not going!"

There was a note of finality in his manner.

It was Maria who brought the news home. The 1961 World Championships were scheduled to take place in Prague. Since this was the year that Maria and Otto had decided to make a bid for the World Pairs Title, Maria was naturally bubbling over with excitement. She already saw herself and Otto in an overseas flight. Father listened intently. Usually any discussion of their skating future aroused his enthusiasm, but now he remained grave. "It is impossible," he added, "The choice of Prague as the site for the World Championships poses not only difficulty but danger. . . ."

Father's refusal made sense. It brought back into sharp focus all the perils we had endured during our flight into exile. It also was a reminder of the dangers any Jelinek might encounter were he foolhardy enough to cross the border into Communist Czechoslovakia.

Red ice was different.

And much, much too thin for the Jelineks.

This was a closed subject, we all realized. In lesser matters, Maria could coax or tease and finally gain her point. But now all of us bowed to Father's decision. Not without grief, though. The following days were grim, not only for Maria and Otto but for the rest of us. The young skaters, being dedicated to the sport of skating, were eager to go. Neither wanted to face the full implications of a return trip to Prague. The house was filled with gloom; the subject wasn't mentioned, but it was evident that we were all immersed in it.

We discovered later that the brooding triggered Father into action. Without confiding in the family, he got in touch with the Minister of Foreign affairs in Ottawa and asked his advice. He had been warned not to send the children to Czechoslovakia for this simple reason: Although we considered ourselves Canadian citizens, to the Czechoslovak regime, we were still Czechoslovak citizens. Taking this into consideration, the Canadian government could do nothing on behalf of Maria and Otto's safety should some mishap occur during their stay in Czechoslovakia. There was only one way out, Father was told, and that would be if the Communist government in Prague released Maria and Otto from their Czechoslovak citizenship.

Then Father got in touch with the International Skating Union in Switzerland, the governing body of the sport. Twenty-eight national associations are affiliated with the Union, whose headquarters is at Davos, Switzerland. He explained that although Canada welcomed us as citizens, it could not keep the Red Czechs from claiming us as theirs. For years, this had caused us no concern, since none of us ever expected to return to our original homeland.

But now Maria and Otto wanted to enter Prague just long enough to lay claim to the World Title in Pairs Figure Skating and bring that title back triumphantly to their adopted homeland.

If the Reds could be persuaded to allow them to enter, it would mean a minor revolution in Prague. The Communists take the dogmatic view that nobody would willingly leave the so-called paradise they had created. Nor did they welcome visitors from the outside world at that time—particularly visitors like the Jelineks, who were expatriots and had such a warm identity with the Czech people.

The Union officials in Davos opened the Jelinek dossier and assembled valid arguments in favor of Father's plan.

The Canadian Skating Association was completely backing the

Jelinek proposals. And what the Jelineks requested was this: Two-way, safe conduct protection, not only to cover Maria and Otto's arrival and stay in Prague but also their journey back home to Canada.

Dr. J. Koch, president, and Herr George Hasler, secretary general of the International Skating Union, were in touch with the Union's liaison officers who, in turn, were in touch with the Czech skating organization. It was thus made clear to the Reds that either the skaters of the Free World, specifically the Jelineks, could come to Czechoslovakia on their own terms or the World Title Championship would take place in another country.

The ultimatum worked.

It is ironic that the final decision by the Prague Reds was influenced by a purely capitalistic motive.

The Communists had already spent millions to arrange for the competition to take place in Prague. Thus, refusal to heed the demands of the Skating Union would result in a great financial loss to Communist Czechoslovakia.

Not that they agreed with grace. They did balk; as a matter of fact, they gave in a few days *after* the deadline for acceptance and just in time to stop the Davos officials from transferring the competitions from Prague to Dortmund in the Rhineland or Cortina D'Ampezzo in Italy.

After this victory, Father, Maria and Otto were summoned to Montreal, where they received the documents that released them from Czechoslovak citizenship. These documents were signed by the Czechoslovak Minister of the Interior. This formality took place before the consul general of the Socialist People's Republic of Czechoslovakia.

The consul himself couldn't have been more courteous and charming. He asked about Maria and Otto's memories of Prague and about their skating plans. As they got up to leave, he wished them good luck, and to the blushing Maria, he added in Czech, "*Ruku libam*," which meant, "I kiss your hand."

It was obvious his sympathies were with the Jelineks. Afterwards, Maria said anxiously that she hoped his courtesy wouldn't lead to his banishment to Siberia.

While they were in Montreal for that meeting with the consul,

Maria and Otto took advantage of the trip to enter the All-Canadian Senior Pairs Competition.

They won. As Canadians! It was a happy omen. Soon they would be upholding their adopted country's banner in Prague.

While a sense of excitement and anticipation is good for any sportsman, since it accelerates the working of his adrenals, it seemed to me there was altogether too much excitement in our home during the following days. Not only were Maria and Otto affected but the rest of our family. This has always been the case with us; what injures one, scars the rest; what gives one joy, infuses the others with a tremendous sense of happiness. But this was really too much. The stars were within our sights; not through a telescope but within grasp.

Lucky Maria and Otto. We basked in their radiance; we lived their dreams with them. The Worlds Title—a dream suddenly with substance.

Skating, like all games, has certain rules and sequences that must be followed. For example, it was essential for Maria and Otto to win the 1961 North American Championships. In Figure Skating, it is an unwritten rule that the contestant, in order to win the World Title, must have won that year either the North American or European Championship. Therefore, to have an opportunity to try for the 1961 World Title, Maria and Otto simply had to place first in the competition scheduled for Philadelphia. Otherwise, they would be forced to wait another two years, since the North American Championships are held only every second year.

Accordingly, Maria and Otto, accompanied by Mother, Bruce Hyland and Jim Proudfoot departed for Philadelphia. Previously, plans for the trip to Prague had come through on schedule. This in itself was, family and friends believed, a good omen. To doting family and friends, it appeared that Maria and Otto were indeed children of destiny.

But the excitement of the past few days had exacted a cruel price from Otto. He was emotionally overstimulated, and the nervous strain manifested itself in a physical illness. When they arrived in Philadelphia, he was ordered to bed and Mother stayed up the entire night with him.

Nevertheless, in the morning, he declared himself perfectly fit. If Maria had doubts, she kept silent, for she had learned it was useless to argue with Otto. Together, they persuaded Mother all was well and proceeded to prove it on the ice.

chapter twelve

INDEED, THEY SKATED BRILLIANTLY ON THE PRAC-
tice days in Philadelphia. Even Bruce seemed drily optimistic.
Twenty-four hours before the Big Day, all of the Pairs Competitors
took to the ice for the last rehearsals, the final striving for the goal
of absolute perfection. Bruce, warmly wrapped, sat in the nearly
empty stadium watching his charges. Otto and Maria were indulg-
ing in a little argument that concerned itself with whatever insig-
nificant faults remained in their technique. Bruce remained silent;
he had no intention, shortly before the event, of disturbing them
with any last minute suggestions. He knew the character of his
charges; nothing short of perfection would suit them and Otto
would be apt to badger Maria into endless hours of rehearsal to
wipe out the faintest flaw Bruce might unearth. The coach was
satisfied. They were at peak form. He sent a wintry smile to Jim
Proudfoot who was huddled beside him. Jim the Jinx, but not
this time. All was well with the young Jelineks.

Out on the rink, Otto said to Maria, "Let's try this lift once
more."

"What, still again?" she demanded. "Why?"

"Don't ask questions. Let's do it."

"Aren't you overdoing it?" she asked. "You know we can do it.
After all, we've been doing it for six years now."

Otto glared at her and then smiled suddenly in entreaty. And

Maria, good sport, devoted sister, took his hand and they were off to repeat the lift.

To Bruce and Jim, the movement was a source of never ceasing awe. Up she soared, serene and confident, in the complicated lift that sent her on a circular flight around Otto's head.

But abruptly, something went wrong. The spectators were too stunned for sound or movement. In a split second, diasaster struck.

Otto's feet lifted awkwardly as Maria reached the summit of the lift.

Otto lost his balance. He fell backwards, landing with an ugly cracking sound on his head.

Maria, from eight feet above, tumbled in a heap on top of him.

A trickle of blood showed against the glittering surface of the ice.

For a long awful moment, everyone seemed frozen into shock. Then a piercing cry from the throat of an American skater released the bystanders from their paralysis. Bruce and Jim rushed over to the fallen skaters. Maria looked up at them dazed. Otto was lying with his eyes closed, a strange pallor on his skin. Blood was oozing from his forehead and down his cheek. He was unconscious.

Maria looked at him. She burst into tears. She tried to get up, and only then realized that she too was badly injured. There was a long deep gash in her thigh where Otto's skate had struck as they fell. Jim Proudfoot lifted her gently to her feet and took her weight on his shoulder as she hobbled to the edge of the ice. Bruce was unaware of anyone but Otto. He was kneeling at Otto's side when the ambulance orderlies arrived, and he remained at Otto's side during the ride to the hospital, with sirens screaming to clear the way.

Maria and Jim followed by car.

Suddenly, the joke that he was the Jelinek jinx was empty of humor.

The telephone rang in Mother's hotel room. She had accompanied Otto and Maria to Philadelphia because of their plans to embark from the States for Prague. It was, she felt, necessary for her to be close to them until takeoff. She was expecting them to call, for the plan was for all of them to have dinner together. So she lifted the receiver in good spirits.

"Hello."

"Hello, Mother, this is Maria."

Mother knew instantly something was wrong; the tension in Maria's voice was the signal. "Is anything the matter?" Mother asked.

"Haven't they told you yet?"

"Told me *what*—? Maria, whatever is wrong—?"

"We're both in the hospital."

Mother was too stunned to find her voice. Maria continued, "I telephoned home and told Father so he'd know about it before the radio broadcasts the news."

She added that Bruce would be coming to fetch Mother to the hospital.

Mother replaced the receiver mechanically. She was drained. Then abruptly, a sense of guilt tightened her heart. Had it been a mistake to shape the lives of her children toward the perfection of their athletic skills? Was she perhaps to blame for this catastrophe?

Fortunately, Bruce arrived before she could lacerate her emotions with these bitter self-accusations.

"Is it bad?" she asked.

"Only God can tell," Bruce answered, and this was to Mother less of a touch of piety than calculated evasion. She thought in a rush of anguish, He knows more than he says! It is bad—But being Mother, she walked without help, her head erect.

To make talk, Bruce said the hospital switchboard had been inundated with calls inquiring about the condition of Maria and Otto.

The sight of Otto shattered Mother; he was lying in bed, his head turbaned with bandages, his skin pallid, his eyes without their usual brightness. Maria reclined in an easy chair, her leg on a stool to ease the throbbing of the deep wound.

"Hello," Maria said with enforced lightness.

"Maria—" For a moment, Mother faltered. At the sound of her voice, Otto opened his eyes. He spoke with an effort.

"We had a fall," he said, and then his voice faded.

Mother panicked. Never before had she known Otto to give in

to pain or illness. Just then, Bruce entered the room with the two doctors who were attending Otto. X rays had been taken; all the tests were accounted for. The neurosurgeon said, "Two weeks of rest are mandatory. Skating is out, of course."

Otto opened his eyes. He said softly, "We're going to skate tomorrow in the competition."

"Impossible. Quite impossible!" The neurosurgeon was no longer young; he was an authority in his field, and this defiance from a half dead patient was outrageous to him. He ran his forefinger over his gray mustache. "My dear young man, you were unconscious for forty-five minutes. When you came to, you had no idea what had happened—or where you were. It is absolutely important to your recovery to rest."

"Do as the doctor asks, Otto," Mother pleaded. "Health is more important than skating."

"Nothing is more important than tomorrow's competition."

"Maria cannot skate tomorrow. She cannot even walk."

"But I can!" Otto's voice was a rebel yell. Whereupon he swung out of bed, tilted himself upon his hands and hand-walked around the room, his bandaged head wobbling uncertainly with his gait.

He passed Maria on the sofa. Instinctively, she moved her leg to give him passage. That faint gesture released the forces of her own will.

"I can walk, too," she announced. And proceeded to do so, but on her feet of course, and limping. She said bravely, "It doesn't hurt a bit."

As soon as she had convinced the others, she sank thankfully again on the sofa. Long afterwards, she confessed to me that those few steps had been sheer torture.

The doctor, unaccustomed to the Jelineks' way of acting, was astounded. He said, somewhat awed, "Amazing. Perfectly amazing!"

The morning of the competition, Maria and Otto held a private conference and decided to go on. Neither Mother nor Bruce could dissuade them. All the skaters did was to make slight readjustments in their routine.

Here is how Jack McKinney described the event in the Philadelphia *Daily News*.

PLUCKY JELINEKS STEAL THE SKATE SHOW.

"The word spread through the 4,026 spectators at the Arena like a breeze riffling through wheat, 'The Jelineks are on the ice.'

"This was the workout period prior to the Pairs Competition in the North American Figure Skating Championships yesterday, and all eyes quickly centered on the trim couple in Cluny brown as they laced through the other pairs on the ice.

"Otto Jelinek's hair had been carefully combed to hide the three stitch wound on his scalp, but a broad strip of bandage was plainly visible on Maria Jelinek's right thigh.

"Injured in a serious practice spill Saturday, the comely brother-and-sister team from Oakville, Ontario, had chosen to ignore the advice of the physician who treated them. Devotees of their refined sport would call this 'pluck.' In the baser sports, it's known as guts.

"Twenty minutes later, the Arena was ringing in tribute to the Jelineks' exciting program of spins, multiple turns, difficult lifts and unison figurations. There would be other champions in the Awards Ceremonies—Laurence Owen of the United States for the Ladies' Singles, Donald Jackson of Toronto for the Men's Singles, Canada's Virginia Thompson and William McLachlan for the Dance Championship. But this day belonged to the Jelineks.

" 'The only thing that worried me was my back,' " Otto Jelinek admitted between congratulations of the other skaters. 'I wrenched it in the spill, and it felt stiff when we first took to the ice. But once I got warmed up, I forgot all about it.'

"A trim twenty-year old whose strength is evident in the slope of his shoulders and the breadth of his neck, Otto bears a three inch scar over his right brow. It's a permanent souvenir of an even more serious practice spill he suffered last year. The Jelineks are a fearless pair and in another sport they'd be called daredevils. 'We talked it over before the competition and made a few adjustments in our program,' said eighteen-year old Maria, who looks anything but devilish off the ice. 'But we eliminated only one lift and it wasn't the one we were injured on. That was such a simple lift,' she added, shaking her head as if she still couldn't understand how the spill had occurred. 'It was just a bit of bad luck—one of those things.' "

What this account neglected to mention was the fact that Maria and Otto were actually awarded four 5.9's and one 6 that day, marks which even champions rarely get, since it indicates one hundred percent perfection. As a matter of fact, any decimal point above five and a half is reckoned a very high marking. They skated with verve and flourish that, for all their injuries, could scarcely be faulted even in tiny details. Only in the evening, during the celebration for them and other skaters in the North American group, did they admit to being exhausted. However, they were happy and relaxed among their friends and fellow skaters. Even Otto's headache and Maria's throbbing leg wound failed to dampen their high spirits.

Suddenly, Dudley Richards, one of the American skaters, suggested, "Why don't we all fly together to Prague?"

"I'd like that very much," Maria said.

Otto agreed. "There's only one problem. If we can change our reservations from the Canadian plane."

"There shouldn't be any difficulty," Dudley said. "Let's hope you can manage it."

"Right," Otto said. "If we don't see you in New York before your take-off, it means we couldn't change our flight."

Maria and Otto left Philadelphia for New York, with Mother and Jim Proudfoot completing their party. Bruce had departed for Toronto early that morning to get his first look at his new son, born as Otto and Maria were winning their championship title. The American skaters were in their own plane, a different flight entirely.

Once at the New York airport, Mother drew Jim Proudfoot aside. "Jim," she said, "please take care of my children. If you can possibly manage it, don't let them out of your sight in Prague."

"Don't worry, Mrs. Jelinek," he promised. "I'll be their watchdog."

Mother turned to Maria and Otto and kissed them. "Good luck. We'll have our fingers crossed."

"Excuse me," Otto said hastily. "We'll have to hurry. I want to see about changing our tickets, so we can fly with the American team."

"Off you go then." Mother turned away, glad that the parting had been so easy. This would be the first competition in which her children would participate without the benefit of her presence. But this competition was to her the most important of all, since it was scheduled in the city barred to her—her beloved Prague.

chapter thirteen

THE SOUND IN THE DAWN AWAKENED ME. IT WAS not the creaking of the old mission walls as the heat rose through the pipes to expand the ancient wood. It was shrill and penetrating; it was, I realized, the telephone. My room is adjacent to the master bedroom, where the upstairs telephone is located, next to Mother's night table. Sitting upright, in a clutch of uneasiness, I listened. The time was a few minutes before five.

"Hello?" It was Mother's voice; no doubt she had automatically picked up the receiver. "Hello? Yes, just a moment, please. He's right here." Then I heard her say to Father, "Some newspaper man from New York wants to speak with you. I didn't catch his name, but he said it was urgent."

Something was grievously wrong; I felt it with all my instincts.

"Hello, Jelinek speaking." Now Father had taken over. "Yes . . . *The New York Times* . . . Oh, they left New York yesterday." Another pause, ominous now; the strain was evident in Father's next words. "One moment, please, while I check with Mrs. Jelinek . . . Jara, what plane did Otto and Maria take for Prague?"

"They were booked to fly with the Canadian skating team," said Mother, "But Otto was trying to switch reservations for the flight carrying the Americans." Her voice grew agitated. "Why? What is it? Is anything wrong?"

Father was talking into the phone again. "We're not sure, but we think they flew with the American team. Why are you asking?"

In the awful seconds of silence that followed his question, I bounded out of bed and into the master bedroom. The light from the bed table lamp accented the pallor on their faces. Father's voice suddenly grew ragged. "They are all dead, you say? All?"

I stared at Mother; she was mute, her face contorted in a spasm of disbelief and horror. Father broke the ghastly silence. He said there had been a plane crash near the Brussels airport. Seventy-three persons were aboard the plane, among them the American figure skating team.

There were no survivors.

No survivors? Did this mean that those warm, lively, gifted young athletes whom Mother had cheered only the day before at the Philadelphia Arena were crushed and bleeding casualties? No survivors.

That meant Otto and Maria . . .

Had they changed their flight to accompany the American team? How could we find out? None of us could speak; we were incoherent. Father switched on the radio. The first broadcast of that long awful day filled the air.

We learned that the plane crashed into a field and burned. It was bound for Prague from New York. Among the dead were Miss Laurence Owen, who had just won the North American Ladies' Figure Skating Championship in Philadelphia. Also the team composed of Mabel Owen, Laurence's elder sister, and Dudley Richards, who had been placed second in Philadelphia. So far as is known, no Canadian skaters were aboard the ill-fated plane."

Father was beside himself. Mother was in shock. She sat immobile and mute. Father projected his anxiety into action. Frantically, he put in a call to Idlewild Airport to seek further information. Waiting was an ordeal.

Finally the news came through. Otto and Maria had evidently stuck to their original plans. They had travelled with the rest of Canada's national team to Prague.

Mother's fervent "Thank God" was mixed with an expression of sorrow for those who were lost. Our gratitude for the safe-keeping of Otto and Maria was touched with an unconscious sense of guilt. God had spared them and there must be an invisible pattern for their good fortune. But even in her gratitude, Mother was sick with anguish for the bereaved parents, who were less fortunate. She kept murmuring to herself, "There must be a reason why they were spared. There must be a reason for this catastrophe. But even though we do not understand, we must not question God's will."

However, the raw throbbing pain of the accident didn't ease during that day as one telephone call followed another.

Richard, who was living in Michigan, telephoned simply to speak with Father. His voice was thick with emotion and he was crying.

"Don't you want to speak to Mother?" I asked.

"What?" he demanded. "Didn't Mother accompany the kids?"

"No she is here. And Maria and Otto are safe in Prague."

"Are you sure?" he asked. "Are you absolutely sure?"

Shortly afterwards, to reassure himself and Mother who was nearly hysterical with renewed anxiety, Father put in a call to Prague. The line to Czechoslovakia's capital was clear. But the calm flat voice of the operator was sickeningly noncommittal.

"Sorry, it is impossible to speak either to Miss Jelinek or Mr. Jelinek. Miss Maria Jelinek is out of town. Mr. Otto Jelinek is seriously ill and no communication is allowed to him."

We were now petrified with terror. For it looked as if Maria and Otto had been lured by false promises of immunity to Prague. We feared they had been arrested by the Communists.

Father sat slumped in his chair. His mood was one of gloom. He blamed himself for his children's plight. Why had he agreed? Why had he even gone so far as to arrange for their return to Prague? On the scales of reality did a skating title balance out this avalanche of grief?

"Those poor children," Mother whispered, and we knew that her tears were not for her own but for those she had bade farewell in New York. "How their parents are suffering . . ."

Watching her, I too, wept, without shame. I looked away, so that my visible grief would not embarrass my father. I went into the bathroom, showered and dressed. But my eyes were swollen and bloodshot, and every so often the tears rolled down my cheeks without control. Since it seemed best to stick to my routine, I went off to school. I was late, but no one censured me. Indeed, as I walked into the classroom, no one dared to look at me. Nor did any of my teachers call on me that day.

At noon, I telephoned home in hope of news. But the air was

gloomy; it looked as though Maria and Otto were under arrest and might indeed be used as hostages. Father had been busy at the telephone all morning, but he had nothing new to report. However, he had contacted Mrs. Hyland at the hospital, and she told him that she expected a call from Bruce at about one o'clock. Hopefully, since he was in Prague, Bruce would have authentic information about my brother and sister.

The afternoon school session was an ordeal. But when I got home, there was waiting for me the first good news of the day. Bruce had been able to telephone. He had seen Maria and Otto only a few minutes before. They were safe and well.

From Bruce, Father learned that Mother was indirectly responsible for the fact that Otto and Maria had joined the Canadian team's flight. Otto's farewell to Mother at the New York airport had delayed him long enough to make a change of reservations impossible. On this thread of fate had their future rested.

Since that day there have been many theories about the cause of the accident. The men in the Brussels control tower saw the erratic flight pattern of the doomed plane and were at a loss for an explanation. What had actually caused "the whole series of spins" which, according to the first news reports, resulted in the plummet to earth that "literally disintegrated" the plane?

Perhaps experts could eventually give the world the cause for the accident. But for us many questions remained unanswered. Why were we given false news about Otto and Maria? And what was the intention behind that Communist lie?

The enigma left Mother uncurious. She shrugged off the suggestion of possible sabotage. All that she was concerned with was the families of the valiant young athletes. She wept for them silently and in her heart until long after the initial horror had eased. We knew that Otto and Maria, too, were in mourning for their friends.

It was through Jim Proudfoot that we learned the details of Otto and Maria's experiences in Prague.

"No cameras now," the stewardess murmured as she moved along the aisle of the plane. "We are over Czechoslovakia and taking pictures is absolutely prohibited." The concern in her voice was genuine, and the passengers had the uncomfortable feeling that some previous passenger had innocently made use of his camera and had been punished.

Jim was accompanying Otto and Maria as a reporter for his paper and incidentally as their protector. He had promised Mother to watch over them and he vowed to keep his promise. He looked out of the plane's window. A half hour earlier they had been flying over the rolling farmland and picturesque villages of Western Germany. Now, the first Communist country he had ever seen unfolded ten thousand feet below him. Was the winter landscape more bleak, or was it merely a trick of his imagination? Was the sky actually grayer? Each village looked like the last; spans of red buildings crowned with yellow roofs. Here and there a muddy road, but without traffic. A stillness. A dullness. A deadness. The plane that an hour ago had been alive with laughter was abruptly a vacuum of silence.

"We should not have come," Otto said.

To hear this utterance from a young man who was the epitome of courage was unutterably depressing to the rest of the team. Suddenly they were conscious of the danger not only for Otto and Maria but for the rest of them. Even for an innocent voyager, there was an awful risk in travelling behind the Iron Curtain. They had all joked about it often enough, but with serious undertones, and the other members of the team were abruptly aware of the truth— that Maria and Otto might be in actual danger.

Since when had the Reds ever kept a treaty or a promise?

"What a story," Jim said, making an awkward attempt to lighten the mood. "You were both born in Prague. You learned to skate there. You escaped. You are coming back now to your original home as ambassadors of Canada, as Canadian champions. You are hot potatoes for the Czechs. They really don't know what to do with you."

"Let them just leave us be," Maria suggested. She looked out of the window, shrugging off the macabre humor of the situation. "I don't like this at all. I wish we'd stayed home."

"I agree," Jim Proudfoot said, feeling quite wretched. "How I agree!"

Their first impression of Czechoslovakia was dismal. The airport was swarming with soldiers and they acted with grim suspicion, as though every passenger was armed to the teeth and determined to capture the city. Nobody smiled.

A sinister looking man in uniform collected their passports as they stepped off the ramp and walked toward the terminal. Giving up the passports was difficult; they seemed to be the team's only link with security.

Jim made it a point to stay close to Maria and Otto. Thus, if anything should happen to them, he thought, he would be a witness. Indeed, had they been taken into custody, Jim would have probably been the third prisoner.

They all sat down to the endless wait while the passports were examined. All of them were conscious of an inability to draw a deep breath; they were suffering from the sense of doom that chills the marrow even on a hot day. Then one of the Czech officials turned and spoke to Maria. She broke into tears.

"Oh, no," she cried, "Surely not all of them!"

To Otto this meant that something must have happened to our relatives in one of the purges that periodically swept the countries behind the Iron Curtain. He felt a sense of sickness at the pit of his stomach. He was convinced they were in serious trouble; that perhaps they would never get out of the country. Silently, he re-echoed Maria's cry, Why had they come here?

The news was finally given to them. It was indeed a catastrophe, much worse than they had imagined. The entire United States Skating team was dead. The tragedy had taken place just about the time the plane with the Canadian team had touched down at Amsterdam.

The shock overshadowed the tension of waiting for the return of their passports. They huddled in a group, too stunned for speech, looking at one another for reassurance, hoping it was all an error in communications, that shortly they would have the reassuring word that it was a mistake.

In the face of such a disaster, the return of their passports brought no elation. They trudged numbly over to the barrier, where, among a few people, a tall erect man waited, a smile on his lips.

"Uncle Jan!" Maria cried in surprise.

It was a Jelinek relative. An official who would drive Maria and Otto to their hotel invited him to join them. The rest of the group would follow by bus.

Shortly afterwards, Jim realized with dismay that his pledge to Mother was already violated. He had allowed the two young Jelineks out of his sight. How did he know this fellow was their uncle? The man said he was; Otto and Maria thought they recognized him as their mother's brother. But he could well be a spy, sent to lure them away from their protectors.

Stop fretting, he scolded himself. He sat back in the bus seat to study the scenery that streamed by. The city of a hundred ancient spires was lovely still, for all the drab atmosphere that enshrouded it. As they approached Prague's New Town, however, Jim realized their ordeal was not yet over.

The previous day, Patrice Lumumba, Communist-influenced rabble-rouser, had been assassinated in the former Belgian Congo. Today, mass demonstrations were scheduled in all the capitals behind the Iron Curtain. The Communists were determined to make Lumumba a martyr. Naturally, western warmongers were accused of his murder.

As the bus lumbered through the streets, the passengers were uncomfortably aware of a strange sight. Thousands of people marching slowly and silently under gigantic banners whose messages needed no translations: "Down with the Imperialists! U.S. Murderers! American War Mongers!" There were posters of the United States flag with knives slashing through the stars and stripes.

Reality calmed the panic in Jim's mind. How could this possibly be a spontaneous demonstration, considering the time and preparations necessary for the parade and posters? But under any circumstances, it was a touchy situation. He wondered uneasily if since their clothing identified them as Westerners, the skating group in the bus might be subjected to physical danger? The travellers decided hastily that should the bus be stopped, they would show their Maple Leaf badges and shout, "Canada! Canada!" in the hope that their country would be held blameless for Lumumba's death.

Later, it became evident to them all that they had generated a good deal of unnecessary anxiety. The marchers were merely performing a boring duty; they were impatient to get it over with and melt away to their homes. As the bus turned into Wenceslaus Square, the demonstrators were left behind and the team proceeded without incident to the Jalta Hotel.

It was soon clear that the guests had little to fear in Czechoslovakia. The hotel staff was friendly and obliging. If not for the gloom cast by the accident to the American team, the Canadian skaters might have thoroughly enjoyed themselves. Besides the cold shocking news from Brussels, the Canadians found themselves the center of interest. Wherever they strolled, crowds gathered, simply to stare at the visitors from the outside world. But in their expressions, Jim, for one, read admiration, sorrow and the despairing resignation of the defeated.

One fact Jim found highly gratifying. There was scarcely a person in Prague who didn't know about Maria and Otto. They were recognized wherever they went. The official story was that the Jelineks were merely of Czech descent. Yet, it seemed that somehow the true story of their background had been passed from person to person, traded in secret, until the young brother and sister had become national heroes.

When Maria and Otto appeared at the ancient Winter Stadium the next morning for a practice session, the crowds were waiting for them. It was never clear to any of the skaters how the people knew when to come. Perhaps they waited all morning with the same endless patience they displayed in queuing up for food and other necessities. They were invariably present, somber and watchful, brightening however, as Maria and Otto displayed their extraordinary skill, laughing and crying at the same time when Maria and Otto replied in Czech to their comments. A glimpse, a brief word, a light touch—these seemed to satisfy the people.

It was not Jim's intention to watch Maria and Otto skate in the Competition. It remained something of a joke with them that whenever Jim was in the audience, they skated less perfectly. Half seriously, half in fun, they still called Jim their jinx.

So Jim decided to spend the time of the finals by himself. He asked Otto to map out a long walk for him in old Prague.

As it turned out, they needn't have gone to the trouble.

Out of deference to the memory of the American victims in the

Brussels crash, the skating championships were cancelled. There was an implied guarantee that the 1962 championships would be re-scheduled in Prague.

Maria and Otto accepted the news with mixed feelings. They truly felt that the competitions should not be held without the United States' skaters. Still they were both at the peak of their training and they were now uncertain whether to continue practice for another year. In every way, it was a depressing letdown.

Nevertheless, while others in the group complained bitterly about the cancellation, Maria said simply, "We've lost only one year of our competitive skating life. The United States skaters have lost their entire lives."

When it was time to leave, Uncle Jan accompanied them to the airport. The farewells were brief.

"Tell Jara that I hope we will see each other again some time," he said. "Tell her that I think constantly of you all."

As the plane was airborne, they saw him still standing at the airport, his heavy coat collar turned up, his face set with the sorrow of the brief reunion and farewell.

"Oh, this crazy world," Maria whispered.

Otto understood her perfectly.

For once he was silent. But he held her hand.

chapter fourteen

L̶OVE DIDN'T ALWAYS WAIT FOR SPRING TO TOUCH
the Jelineks with its magic.

My brothers and sister are touchingly suggestible to romance;
it is due, Father often says wrily, to the emotional Czech genes.
Richard, the quiet, reticent scholar, was, curiously enough, the
first of the sons to fall seriously in love. Not that we were aware
of it. Unlike the rest of us, Richard often hides his feelings to save
himself from family comments, which can be blistering.

Perhaps Richard, more than the rest of us, felt the need to
establish himself in Father's eyes as a mature man. To prove his
worth, he started his own business shortly after graduation from
high school in the summer of 1956. Father, delighted with his
scholarly son's unexpected interest in business, underwrote the
project and thus Richard founded the R. J. Assembly.

The factory was established in an abandoned chicken coop,
which he renovated. Richard proved himself to be a responsible
"industrialist." Each morning he got up at 3:30 to light the furnace
in his little workshop. He was only nineteen, but he had inherited
the Jelinek zest for living, which included the ability to celebrate
until dawn and then put in a day's work.

About three dozen women worked for him, producing decanter-
tops for Christmas merchandise, and they adored and pampered
him. They were heartbroken when, before Christmas, the "plant"
closed down for the season, and Richard embarked for Europe. It

was his plan to learn something about the cork business in Portugal and Spain; at least, that was the obvious reason for his trip. And he did spend several weeks in cork factories, before he and a high school friend decided to tour through Europe. However, he returned to Canada much earlier than anticipated. His interest in blondes had focused on a high school classmate, and none of the sights of old world grandeur could compensate for the fact that he missed her acutely.

He returned to Oakville quite the man of the world—in his own nineteen year old mind. Whereupon he presented Father with an ultimatum. He would bypass college and come immediately into the family business.

Father was outraged.

Richard was adamant.

They are both obstinate; each finds it impossible to give in gracefully first, so the summer dragged by in a battle of wills. Father was pleased with Richard's maturity but he suspected there was an amorous motive back of his son's sudden determination to turn businessman. Particularly since Richard was so obviously academically oriented. They reached no clear cut decision—Frank remained in the background; Mother tried, without success, to mediate. A compromise was established. That summer of 1957, Richard settled in Lockport, New York, where Frank was managing Father's cork factory. It was agreed that Richard would be Frank's assistant. While Richard was there, his basic need to study reasserted itself, and he enrolled at night school in the University of Buffalo. It was primarily a gesture to show Father he knew his own mind; nevertheless, it proved to be the first important step in Richard's future.

It's strange how often we Jelineks have initiated projects to prove ourselves to Father, and then discovered we have immeasurably helped ourselves.

Already, Richard's extraordinary power of concentration and unflagging energy were evident. He would work in Lockport until closing time, hastily swallow a sandwich and take off for Buffalo, some twelve miles distant. There he would attend classes for three or four hours, after which he would return to Lockport, do his home work, and snatch what sleep he could.

Weekends, he drove back to Oakville, not only to visit his family but the girl who had captivated him. Her name was Elizabeth Nelson and she was a radiant blonde whom Richard had met at the local high school. She was seventeen the summer of 1958 and Richard was twenty-one, and like all young lovers, they found separation from each other unbearable. Particularly since in February of that year Richard had enrolled as a transfer student at the University of Michigan. Liz's parents encouraged the marriage for they felt their daughter was sufficiently mature in spite of her age to know what she was about. Mother and Father, however, felt that if Richard were committed to the responsibilities of marriage, he might never complete his college education.

That year, Otto and Maria were sent to a private school in Davos, Switzerland. I was plugging away at school in Oakville. Frank covered us all with glory by falling in love with a radiantly beautiful and gentle English girl, Patricia Smith, who had recently moved to Oakville. In conjunction with Father's two cork factories, Frank now established his own business, Jelinek Sports, Limited. He was well able to support a family.

Liz and Richard were part of Patricia and Frank's wedding party and the occasion evidently was contagious. For although Richard had agreed to finish college before marriage, he gave Liz a diamond ring that night. Richard was somewhat depressed to return to Michigan still a bachelor; in January 1959, to our surprise, he announced that he and Liz had decided to break their engagement. It was a time of confusion at home. Our parents were divided in their feelings. They wanted Richard to be happy, naturally, but they knew how important education was to a young man of his nature. To prove how reasonable he could be, Father promised Richard that once he graduated and Liz completed her high school education, he would underwrite their honeymoon —a month in Europe and a new car. It did not seem too much to ask of the young couple, since Father stressed that it was for their own good.

Love and mathematics were warring in Richard's blood. He had promised Father to wait. But Liz was young and lovely, and the memory of her was constantly tormenting him. That summer,

Oakville held no happiness for him; not even Michigan satisfied his needs. A lovely feminine vision blocked his mind. At Father's suggestion, he flew out to Colorado Springs to take a job at the Broadmoor Hotel. Father and Mother figured that a change of atmosphere and the bracing mountain air and new interests might do him good.

Richard arrived in Colorado Springs fortified with letters of introduction to top men in the hotel business. But true to form, he didn't use them. Instead, he applied for any job available and became a bus boy. His pay was 89 cents per hour, plus tips.

Being on his own was a heady experience. He decided it was an auspicious omen. Whereupon he rented a small furnished apartment, put in a long distance call to Liz and proposed marriage.

"What about your schooling?" Liz asked.

"I'll make it," Richard said. "I'll show Father I can do it my way."

This was all the encouragement Liz needed. Clutching a corsage of white roses, Richard met her at the airport, and they were married on Thursday, June 25, 1959, at the Chapel of the First Methodist Church in Colorado Springs.

Once the honeymoon was over, they set out to demonstrate that marriage and college were compatible.

At the end of August, they left Colorado Springs, feeling unbelievably happy and with their purse filled with three hundred dollars savings. They drove to Michigan in two days to save on motels, arrived in Ann Arbor in the early afternoon, found an apartment that evening and set up light housekeeping.

Although Liz had only a few months of business school, she was able to get a good job in the Mechanical Engineering Department of the University. They decided Richard must not work that year since his studies were so demanding. They had some small income from Richard's investments and this, together with Liz's salary, seemed to be adequate.

Father was depressed and pessimistic.

Liz confided to Mother that she was positive they would be successful. There was the extra incentive of proving they could accomplish what has become a routine challenge for many contemporary young couples, but has been a source of astonishment to our parents. In the Czechoslovakia of their youth, young couples didn't embark on marriage under such impulsive and precarious circumstances.

Liz is a gay animated girl, but I've always suspected the Jelinek family is a source of puzzlement to her. Often she seems to feel it necessary to guard her individuality with extraordinary and defensive zeal.

I don't blame her for taking delight in pointing out that before marriage Richard's grade point average was relatively low. After marriage it rose several points each semester until he finished his undergraduate work with an overall B average. He received a tuition scholarship and was elected to Alpha Pi Mu, the Industrial Engineering Honor Society. He also received a commendation from the President's Committee on Employment of the Handicapped in Washington for his design of a stair climbing wheelchair. In February, 1961, Richard received his bachelor's degree in Industrial Engineering.

Both Liz and Richard found enormous satisfaction in demonstrating to skeptics, particularly Father, that they could achieve marriage and academic success simultaneously. There is no doubt in our minds that the need to prove Father wrong was a tremendous impetus in Richard's career.

"No matter how exasperated I'd get," Liz once confided to me, "I had to admit that the contribution of Richard's parents was most effective. Mother Jelinek is always so kind and ready to listen, and Father Jelinek, for all his gruff exterior, wanted only the best for his family. As a result, he concentrated on keeping Richard on the path leading to his individual goal. Whenever Richard strayed from the main road, Father Jelinek was there to direct him back." Liz looked rather wistful, but she added staunchly, "Richard's parents are certainly responsible for the trait which seems to dominate the family—to strive for the best."

Once again, that reminder—the pursuit of excellence.

In February, 1958, Maria had her first taste of love.

In many ways, she was still a child, with glowing cheeks, flying pigtails, sound appetite, her habits as healthy as a young athlete's should be. Yet the budding femininity showed itself in her room with its collection of dolls from all parts of the world and the stuffed animals that cuddled on her bed. In some ways, however, she was sophisticated; she was already an experienced world traveller. She adored travel, which was usually an ordeal for Mother since Maria insisted on taking the contents of her room with her. Maria is so much like our mother. Outwardly she is serene and self contained; inwardly she is full of tensions. From Mother, she has picked up the habit of shredding a bit of paper. But if you ask, "Maria, are you nervous?" she turns on the flood-lights of her eyes and says simply, "No, I am not nervous."

Nevertheless, if our parents are in the audience, something is apt to go wrong on the ice.

Maria and Otto try too hard.

Father concedes with indulgent pride that Maria is stubborn. When she wants something, she gets it in her quiet intense way. She is adored by her brothers; yet as a small girl, she used to wait on Frank and share chores with Richard. Among the skaters, who are a notoriously self-centered group, she is given complete love. The "rink rats," who clean the ice, adore her. She has a kind word for everyone; status doesn't impress her in the least. In 1963, when she was starring in Ice Capades, and heard that the bosses were seated down front, she said serenely, "I couldn't care less. I can't do any better than I've been doing. So why should their presence upset me?"

This air of equanimity didn't hold true of our sister that winter month in 1958. Our parents were in Paris with Maria and Otto, who were appearing in the World Skating Competition.

Even in February, Paris has something for young lovers. It is the magical quality in the air, the special radiance that the city reserves for the young and vulnerable. Maria was scarcely sixteen, her tomboy years not too far behind her. But suddenly, during that skating competition, she began to blossom. Our parents were aware of it; Otto was aware of it, but by some inner tact they kept silent and watched the unfolding of the feminine heart. Maria's hair took on a lovely luster; her skin was like porcelain with a blush of rose; her eyes were filled with dreams.

The reason for the miracle was to be seen each day on the skating rink. His name was Boris. He was eighteen and the Russian Singles Champion.

Mother has said since, that never before had she been witness to a young love so touching in its candor and innocence. It was an exquisite idyl. It was incidentally Maria's first realization that a boy could be more than a brother.

Maria wanted only to talk about Boris.

She said to Father, "I didn't sleep all night."

"Why not, Maria?"

With her eyes so luminous, her candor so shattering in its simplicity and depth, she said, "Boris held my hand."

It was in its way a version of Romeo and Juliet, circa 1958.

It was a risk for Boris even to sit near Maria in the rink, for the Russian skaters were carefully supervised.

Yet once or twice they stole away and walked in the Tuileries.

She was skating only for him.

He was skating only for her.

When they had to say goodbye, Boris leaned down and kissed her on the forehead. He gave her a primitive Russian doll as a memento. It has a place of honor in the cabinet in her bedroom.

They never saw each other again.

Now Maria has many suitors.

"He is too tall," she says of one. "He is too short," she says of another. "He wears odd clothes," she says of a third. "He cannot talk my language," she says of a fourth.

First love can be beautiful and painful and a never to be forgotten experience. None of us knows what goes on in Maria's heart. She is gay and lively and funny and superb, and when she is at home, she helps Mother serve dinner and often they meet in her room for girls' talk.

But Boris is never mentioned.

chapter fifteen

A YEAR HAD PASSED SINCE THE TRAGEDY THAT befell the American Skating Team.

For Maria and Otto, it had been a year of hard dedicated work. They were back in the grinding practice sessions, the endless battle with muscle fatigue, weariness and the elusive goal of perfection. Now they were inspired with a burning mission—to win not only for themselves but in memory of their cherished friends.

So it was a kind of second act when in 1962 Maria and Otto, accompanied once again by Bruce Hyland and Jim Proudfoot, returned to Prague. It was as though the intervening months had been an over-long intermission. The cast that assembled was similar—skaters from all over the world. The backdrop was the same, the Winter Stadium and the twisting fairy tale streets of old Prague.

The 1962 World Championships were once again scheduled for Prague. This fact was established early the previous autumn. During the twelve month interval, Maria and Otto had lost none of the skill, ambition and will that Bruce counted on. Incredible as it might seem, their skating had actually improved. They had acquired a glittering self assurance and poise, that, combined with their extraordinary skill, made them an irresistible force in the arena. Bruce said he could scarcely wait to get to Czechoslovakia.

"Neither can we," Otto replied with wry humor.

Indeed, they were all cheerful about the prospect of the second trip to Prague. They knew what to expect. They were confident that they understood the Czech character and the knowledge warmed their hearts.

Their brief visit the previous year had taught them an unforgettable lesson about people. The human spirit is invincible in the face of discouragement and oppression. When they had first stepped off the plane, their impression was of a people that never smiled. Yet during the 1961 stay, they found in private audiences the grim mask of bleak resignation melted and the warm personality of the Czechs emerged. They discovered that the national attributes of gaiety and good manners and cheerful hope were able to withstand the hundred forms of cruelty that life assumed under the Communist yoke. In spite of all subjugation, the joyous Czech personality continued to flourish.

"I am beginning to understand the Czechs," Jim Proudfoot said, as they landed once again at the Prague airport. "Their spirit thrives under the most impossible circumstances, without nourishment of any kind, fighting like a brave blade of grass that sprouts through a crack in the cement walk."

"The Jelineks will win. The Jelineks must win!"

Wherever a couple of Czechs met in private, these words summed up the essence of their feelings. Although the Communist press printed reluctantly a story about Maria and Otto, there was no mention of the family escape. Nevertheless, all of Prague was aware of it. The Jelinek story was whispered on street corners, in restaurants, in homes. The citizens of our homeland said silent prayers for Otto and Maria. Now, more than ever before, they were a symbol of freedom.

The Jelinek story had been big in 1961, but it was even more important in February of 1962, as the world was coming out of the frozen winter. Having lived through so much of the saga, Jim Proudfoot declared he simply had to be in on the ending.

"This is a rare moment," he told his Toronto editor, "the sort of experience that comes only once in a lifetime."

When his newspaper hesitated about underwriting the assignment, Jim arranged for a week's vacation and booked his own passage to Prague. He had no intention of missing the final chapter of this drama. Subsequently his intuition was vindicated.

His editors were delighted to buy his dispatches, as the Jelinek saga unfolded.

He was late in leaving Toronto. Otto and Maria were already in Geneva, working diligently on the final polishing of their five minute competitive routine. Just before Jim took off from home, there had been a desperate call from Switzerland. Otto had broken a skate blade and was leaving for Czechoslovakia without a spare. The gamble was much too great. Some means had to be found to get a duplicate as quickly as possible to Prague from a renowned blades skate maker in Syracuse.

It was indeed a stroke of fortune that Jim had not been able to leave with Otto and Maria. The duplicate skates weren't even ready when he took off from New York. They were late in arriving in London, where he spent a few days; as a matter of fact, the skates arrived only the morning he left London for Prague.

At customs in Prague, however, he was uncomfortably aware of the curious package the skates made. The inspector's look was glacial. All of Jim's former apprehensions rushed back, leaving him with a sickish feeling in the pit of his stomach. He remembered the admonitions of his Toronto travel agent, who warned him about the hazards of trying to outwit any government behind the Iron Curtain. There was no more foolhardy blunder, she had cautioned him, than to try to smuggle an object in or out of the country. The police needed only an excuse to lock up a traveller. The fact that the previous year Jim had successfully emerged from Prague carrying Father's vast stamp collection did little to improve his peace of mind as the inspector examined the hard little package.

"What is this?" the man demanded suspiciously.

"Skates." Jim described a double axel with his hands. "Otto Jelinek."

"Yes, yes." Gold fillings flashed as the inspector suddenly smiled. "*Sourozenci Jelinkovi—dobre, dobre.*"

He waved Jim on as if he were carrying a message from the Kremlin.

Jim found a taxi to transport him to downtown Prague, where the Jalta Hotel was situated. Here he was greeted by the staff like an old friend. The porter puffed out his cheeks and chided him for gaining weight since the previous year. As Jim listened to the chatter of Czech words from all sides, the ones he recognized clearly were the names of Maria and Otto. During lunch at the Jalta, the waiter asked him in excellent English whether the Jelineks would be at the hotel. Jim couldn't promise since the skaters were all staying at the International which was across the city. In the elevator, the operator thrust a photograph at him and asked if the Jelineks could be persuaded to autograph it.

Thus Jim found himself a small-time celebrity merely because he was known to be a friend of the young skaters. This to him was an indication of the high level of excitement that permeated the city.

Later that first evening, he asked a porter to summon a cab to take him to the International Hotel. When the porter accompanied him to the taxi and opened the door for him, the conversation between the two Czechs was literally peppered with mentions of the Jelineks.

As the cab bounced over the cobblestones of Wenceslaus Square, in the deepening night, Jim tried to visualize what this city had been like a quarter of a century ago. Prague was then among the world's brightest and most sophisticated capitals. But now, only an occasional pedestrian scurried by, appearing briefly in the dim, widely spaced street lights then blending into the shadows. Automobiles were rarely seen. Only the wonderful antique street cars, clanging bravely, brought a touch of relief to the gloom.

Three days before, Jim had been walking in Piccadilly Circus. The contrast between the two was shattering. For Jim knew there had been a time when Wenceslaus Square had outshone Piccadilly Circus and most of the other famous squares of the world.

It didn't seem incongruous that the only sign of real life was in the bars. They were all crowded. A bar, Jim reflected, had validity for two reasons—either because you were celebrating or you needed to escape the bleak realities of your existence. The true reason was self-evident this night in Prague.

At the bottom of the Square, which is a half mile from the ancient museum that dominates the plaza, the cab stopped dutifully for a red light. There wasn't another car in sight, but the driver waited, abruptly wheeled right and proceeded through a smaller square that was surrounded by gigantic posters extolling the People's Republic. Finally, they crossed the Moldau River. Down to the right on its island squatted the old Winter Stadium, built decades before by Zizka. On the left Jim could distinguish the towers of Charles Bridge and above, outlined in the thickening gloom, the Hradcany Castle and St. Vitus Cathedral, relics of a happier time.

Finally, they passed through a tunnel and emerged on the upper plain where the newer part of Prague is situated. A few blocks farther on at the International Hotel, he found Maria and Otto waiting. In spite of the fact that the Competitions were ahead of them, they were in jaunty spirits.

Jim saluted them with mock gravity. "You are such celebrities here," he said, "I'm grateful that you can spare me a few minutes of your precious time."

They burst into laughter and embraced him fondly.

Dear Jim Proudfoot.

Darling Jim the Jinx.

"It's terrible," Maria said. "The phone never stops ringing. So many invitations, and it's so hard to say *no*."

"I've told you many times," Jim said patiently, "if you're going to be famous, you'll have to learn to be impolite. There just isn't enough time to be nice to everybody."

"But we owe it to these people," Otto reminded him. "The whole thing means so much to them."

"Besides," added Maria, "so many of them are our relatives."

"Or say they are," Jim said.

"There was a note under our door when we checked in," Otto related. "It said, 'Show them you can win. Please do it for us—your friends.' How can we let them down?"

"You can't, of course," Jim replied, "and you'd better not."

Maria tucked her legs under her, as she curled up on the armchair; they were seated in her room, away from prying eyes and curious ears.

"They keep coming up to us on the street," she said. "Strangers. But they all say the same thing—we've got to win. They are praying for us. Imagine that, praying for us. We can't even take a walk without something like that happening."

Jim couldn't help but be concerned. The pressure was building up for Maria and Otto during that week before the Competitions. It wasn't good for them. And yet, it was easy for him to appreciate the circumstances that motivated the Prague citizens. Isolated, worlds away from a normal civilized life of freedom, they felt that the entire universe was narrowed until the competition, with those five minutes of concentrated effort, assumed a proportion so vast and encompassing that it blotted out all else. If the Czechs had lost their sense of proportion, who could blame them?

Jim stayed longer than he had originally intended with Maria and Otto. He was reluctant to leave them. Mother's admonition from the previous year still lingered in his mind. "Don't let my children out of your sight," she had begged. Well, they were a year older and circumstances had changed somewhat so they were reasonably safe in Prague, he reflected. If any harm should come to them, Prague might be witness to a new kind of uprising. For they were already entrenched in the hearts of their former compatriots. Still, he wasn't comfortable.

After he sent them off to bed, Jim had a beer at the penthouse bar and then awakened the dozing desk clerk.

"Is it possible to summon a cab?" he asked.

"Certainly," the clerk replied. "But you must wait. It will be several minutes before a car arrives."

There was a pause.

"You are an American, sir?"

"No, Canadian," Jim replied. "A journalist."

"Of course! The Jelineks." The man behind the desk added, "Sir, I wonder if you would accept a small gift to take back to Canada with you."

Without waiting for a reply, he produced a postcard with a colored drawing of a fat sleepy looking soldier. "It's Schweik," he said. "You know the story of Schweik, do you not?"

Jim had heard it often from Father but he said with compassion, "No, I'm afraid not," for it was evident the man had a great need to unburden himself.

Schweik, the clerk explained eagerly, was again the hero of Czech folklore, just as he had been a generation ago. Schweik was compelled to enter the army during World War I. He obeyed, but he was so slow and stupid, his mistakes seemed so sincere, that his officers were driven to madness. Yet he could never be accused of direct disobedience or disrespect.

"Today we are a nation of Schweiks," the man said, adding quietly, "I was not always a clerk."

For the first time, Jim looked closely at him, noting his chiselled features, his carefully groomed silver hair, the vague atmosphere of faded elegance.

"I am sorry—" Jim said.

The older man came back to reality. "Ah, I talk too much sometimes. I must be getting old. Besides, I believe your taxi is ready now."

The following morning, Maria, Otto and Jim were involved in a riot.

It happened while they were out on a shopping expedition. Jim said, "It is my conviction that the finest product of Czechoslovakia is its Pilsen beer."

"That may be," Maria agreed serenely, "but I want some crystal to bring home to Mother."

There was a valid reason for them to buy Czech products. Maria and Otto had been paid for a series of scheduled exhibitions. The bulk of the money they had turned over to relatives, but they still had a supply of Czech crowns to spend in Prague. Back in Canada the money would be worthless, except to collectors of coins.

Accordingly, they decided to visit Prague's finest crystal shop, just around the corner from Wenceslaus Square. Jim waited for Otto and Maria to pick him up at the Jalta; as they began to walk, crowds collected and followed them.

Maria and Otto were both pleased and embarrassed. Although by then they were minor celebrities accustomed to jousting with admiring mobs, they had never before encountered anything quite like this avalanche of adoration. How do you have the heart to elude people who look at you with that special love and grace? So, shy but smiling, Maria and Otto entered the crystal shop, followed by the crowd. Immediately, passers-by, attracted by the commotion, peeped into the store windows and recognizing the young stars, jammed in. Everyone was babbling simultaneously; some raised autograph books, others pads or scraps of paper for the

Maria and Otto practicing in Prague (1962).

Signing autographs on the streets of Prague.

Before the old Jelinek house, now the Austrian
Legation.

Soldiers and skaters.

Sharing memories with an old friend.

Triumphant return to Canada; Oakville welcomes Maria and Otto.

Champions of the World!

Jelinek inscription. It was growing hot, and the managers became anxious not only for the young Jelineks but for the fragile merchandise.

His fear proved valid. A couple of figures were brushed off a showcase, shattering on the floor. Then, with a splintering crash an entire counter was toppled. More people crowded into the tiny establishment. Otto and Maria were jammed against a wall by their frenzied admirers. People were shoving each other. Another showcase crashed. There were cries of pain. The trio was terrified that there would be casualties. They looked for an exit.

The manager, flushed, perspiring profusely and ragged with nerves, elbowed his way to the door and shouted for a policeman. Two came in and quickly established order. The manager hung a sign on the door, which Maria, with delicious humor read: "It says 'Out for Lunch.' " The Jelineks recompensed the shop-keeper for the damage, and then continued their shopping in peaceful privacy.

Mother got her choice crystal.

Between practice sessions, Otto suggested, "Let's take a look at our old home."

"No," Maria said and pain shadowed her clear bright eyes. "I'd rather not."

"Oh, come along," Otto teased. "Aren't you curious?"

They invited Jim to accompany them. The sprawling old mansion that was once our home had been first seized by the Reds. Shortly afterwards, it became the Austrian Embassy. The trio found their way to their old house without difficulty. As they paused before the enormous timbered front door, Maria said softly, "If only Father and Mother could be with us."

"And Frank and Richard and Henry," Otto added.

He picked up the knocker and let it fall against the ancient wood.

"Perhaps we shouldn't disturb them," suggested Maria, who would never willingly disturb anyone.

"Don't be silly," Otto retorted. Never diffident, he added, "It's our home, anyway."

But there was no answer. Otto, however, was not deterred. "We'll try again," he decided.

The following day he led Maria and Jim, with an uncanny recollection of streets he had once prowled, fourteen years before, as a small boy. A streetcar carried them across the Moldau, twisting back and forth through a web of crooked cobblestone streets. Finally, Otto commanded with a glint in his eyes, "Everybody off!" Jim and Maria followed him. "These stairs will take us up to the castle," he announced; and so they did, the broad stone steps, smoothed by centuries of traffic, affording them an expanding view of the Old Town as they reached the top.

"Once I ran down these stairs as fast as I could," said Otto, "and hit a stone sticking up. I rolled down the rest of the way. The scars are still on my knees."

As they reached the top landing and stepped into the Square, Maria recalled their visit there the previous year as passengers on a sightseeing bus. They dashed across the plaza and along the street that was familiar to sure-footed Otto. They reached the stone mansion and he knocked on the heavy door.

This time, it creaked slowly open and they were greeted by an elderly woman with a careworn face.

"Hello," Otto began, "I am—"

Before he could finish his introductions, the woman caught him in a warm enveloping embrace. Then she extended her loving arms to Maria. Her lined face was smiling, even while tears spilled over.

"Otto and Maria," she exclaimed. "My children. We often told ourselves you would come home again—"

She was Pepi. "You remember me?" She was begging for recognition. "I used to bathe and feed you and take you for your walks—"

"Pepi, of course!" Otto said, "Pepi, our nurse."

"Come in, come in," she begged, "*Come home!*"

She had been with our family until we went into exile. Later, she returned to serve in a similar capacity for the Austrian ambassador who now occupied the house. The ambassador and his family were out of town, but they had left instructions with the staff that if Otto and Maria called, they were to be made welcome.

The house was familiar to Otto and Maria; old memory patterns returned quickly. But to Jim Proudfoot, the place was an example of old world elegance. The street door deposited the visitor in a cool passageway that opened to a sweep of magnificent gardens. To the left, the circular staircase made a stunning backdrop for the hall and the spacious main rooms. Otto and Maria, hand in hand, bounded up the stairs.

"This was our living room," Otto announced to Jim. "You see, our piano is still here."

"I remember one night when our parents were giving a party," Maria interjected, "I was dying with curiosity, so I came down-stairs in my nightdress and watched. I was very small but the men treated me like a young lady. They bowed and kissed my hand."

Otto strode through another doorway. "I don't think the li-brary's been changed at all," he said as they trotted after him. "Yes, here are the silk draperies Father chose to please Mother!"

The library was indeed unchanged; the bookcases crammed with the family's favorite volumes; the fine old carved desk; the paintings; even the rare Persian rugs. Jim was entranced. He told us later that he tried to visualize what an evening in that house must have been like during the splendid pre-war days—the logs crackling in the vaulted fireplaces, the lilting music from the quartet of players on the balcony; the laughter; the elegance of the women in Paris gowns and the men in their formal attire. It was no wonder, Jim reflected, that Father had been a prime target for both Nazis and Communists. Jim realized then that there were kinds of heartbreak and stress that the sheltered North American mind simply cannot encompass.

They mounted the staircase that led to the sleeping quarters.

"Frank nearly killed himself on these stairs," Otto recalled. "He slid down, using a rocking chair as a toboggan."

And so it went. The present encouraged memories of the past with aching poignancy. Here was the room where the older boys had slept and where Richard had prepared his brothers for the flight to Switzerland. There was the gymnasium where Father had established the athletic prowess of his family. And the vast master bedroom, where the Communist plunderers had so badly fright-ened Mother. The three of them wandered through the garden like children in a fairy tale. They found the tree Otto had used as a battle station to hurl green apples at a Communist official. Jim realized how difficult it was for Maria and Otto to bid farewell to Pepi and the others on the staff and the lovely old house.

As they left, Jim turned automatically to the left end of the road. Otto paused suddenly, his brow wrinkled.

"Let's go another way," he said. "It's shorter and it will take us to the Old Town Square, where Father's office used to be."

So they retraced the route Father and Otto once followed on those special days when Otto was permitted to visit the office. Otto now led them confidently through the labyrinth of the Old Town. They turned another corner and emerged in the Square, perhaps the oldest section of the ancient city. It was nearly four in the afternoon, and they joined the crowd gathered to watch the spectacular clock on the Town Hall tower strike the hour. Sure enough, promptly at four, the mechanized procession of kings and gnomes, saints and ogres, soldiers and witches filed out of the clock in the formal rites that had been initiated centuries ago.

Otto reminded them of the story of the great artist who had created this major work. When it was completed, King Wenceslaus ordered the man blinded, so he would never duplicate his master-pieces. Yet a copy had been made eventually, since the original clock was destroyed at the end of World War II, when Prague was in revolt against the Nazis.

"The rebuilding of this relic is one of the rare praiseworthy acts I came across behind The Iron Curtain," Jim later commented.

When it rains in Moscow, the saying goes, they carry umbrellas in Prague. This is a valid assessment of the Soviet influence in Czechoslovakia. Yet Maria, Otto and Jim all felt that it was impossible to visit these people and not leave with a feeling other than confidence that one day the old democratic regime must return. Behind the mask of sorrow laced with laughter, there was a deep rooted purpose, a tough core of pride which promised the Communist that the passive rebellion of the Good Soldier Schweik would eventually run its course. And that the people would rise once more in a torrential wave to overcome the tyrants.

Victory for the young Jelineks therefore would be less of a vindication than the promised dream of liberation.

chapter sixteen

So here it is, March 14, 1962, the Great Day, with all the disappointments, setbacks, quarrels, tears, toil and laughter that hid sorrow behind them.

Behind them, too, is the tumble that may have ruined their chances for the Championship. However, the thousands of rooters who are jammed into the stadium cannot accept the possibility of their failure. Over and over, there is a low chant:

"Today this nation has one motto,
The victory of Maria and Otto."

Thousands of pairs of eyes are focused on the judges. In his seat, Jim prays fervently, Let it be! Let it be! He looks at Otto and Maria, outwardly so composed and smiling as they make their bows to the adoring audience. Bruce is inscrutable, but Jim is aware of his sick tension. There is a ripple of expectation from the audience as the judges arise. The arena grows silent. All eyes are strained toward the judges. Otto and Maria stand at the edge of the ice, nervous, expectant. Both Jim and Bruce are poised with pencil and pad to mark down the scores.

Good marks from the Austrian judge. A sigh of relief from the audience. A win there.

Low marks from the Canadian. But nothing to be concerned about, since all of his marks have been on the low side.

Excellent marks from the Czech. A possibility.

The East German judge is enthusiastic. A chance there.

A disappointment from the West German judge, who incredibly placed the Jelineks below that nation's second string pair.

Support from Great Britain.

And from Switzerland.

And from the U.S.A.

The Russians—again a low score, below the West Germans.

Trouble.

Now they must wait it out; patience and prayer.

Belousova and Protopopov had skated beautifully. Jim totalled up the marks and according to his calculations, Otto and Maria had ranked first by the judges from Austria, Canada, East Germany, Great Britain and the United States. Shaking with excitement, he rushed down to the dressing room. He collided in the corridor with Bruce Hyland. Each held out his score card. They tallied.

"We've made it," Jim shouts.

Otto looked out of the dressing room. He said, "Don't get excited. You guys are always wrong."

Under any circumstances, however, the job is done.

The announcement rang through the stadium. It detonated an avalanche of stupendous and overwhelming emotion.

"Ladies and gentlemen," the Czech marshal began, "it is my pleasure to announce that the World Pairs Champions and the winners of the gold medals are the *sourozenci*—"

Sourozenci!—

Brother and sister, siblings, whatever the word meant in native Czech, the young Jelineks knew they had won. So did the audience, even before the formal announcement was fully uttered. It was not only for their superb technical skill, which seemed to defy the laws of nature, not only for their graceful indifference to the principles of centrifugal force, but for the shining spirit, the marvelous inner core of devotion to an art, a discipline and a belief.

The response from the audience was a tremendous roar, a wild jubilant ovation such as few had ever before witnessed. That emotional response was a great vital force that swept up audience and performers in its tumultuous path. Usually, as soon as the results are announced in a skating contest, most people leave in order to avoid the rush. But this time, people remained by their seats. The cheering continued, growing to a magnificent crest, like the great waves breaking on shore.

Maria and Otto responded simply to the avalanche of hand-clapping. They skated out on the ice, circled the rink, finally gliding off each on one foot, their left hands joined, Otto's right hand on Maria's waist. They went around once and then again and the applause rose to thunder. Then the excited supercharged mob leaped the barriers and surged onto the ice, cheering wildly.

"We have won!" they cried, many in tears, "We are the World Champions!"

It began to look as though Maria and Otto would never be allowed to depart. Finally, they were spirited out of a back door and driven back to the hotel. Usually, there are celebrations after a championship contest. But that night, Maria and Otto had a bite to eat at the hotel and went to their separate rooms. There was no energy left to celebrate; the extraordinary reception had drained their emotions. In a quiet way, they knew this was the greatest victory they would ever enjoy.

Maria fell asleep immediately. Otto did not sleep that night at all. He roamed around his room and at about five in the morning, he looked out of the window and saw hundreds of people on their way to work. In Czechoslovakia, the work day in factories and offices begins at six A.M. It reminded him of the early morning practice sessions back home in Canada.

All the European major newspaper correspondents were in the arena. In their exuberant reports, they all emphasized the fact that the Czechs considered Maria and Otto's victory their victory. In the report that special correspondent Horst S. Vetten sent to his newspaper, *Die Welt,* he wrote:

"He was pale, almost ashen—his expression cold. She had red cheeks and smiled. Otto Jelinek stared unseeingly, as if he had problems to solve all the time. Maria Jelinek looked merrily around waving as she did so. Half the crowd waved back excitedly.

" 'Here they are,' " the Czech next to me said unnecessarily.

"The Jelineks made way for the German pair, Franz Ningel and Margret Gobl, who had just finished their routine, and were leaving the ice. Maria Jelinek stroked the cheek of the German girl in a friendly gesture. Otto Jelinek absent-mindedly shook hands with Franz Ningel and murmured something unintelligible.

" 'They have arrived,' " exclaimed my neighbour, continuing his strange monologue.

"Now he suddenly sat bolt upright, intent and eager, and looked down at the ice-surface. Prior to this moment he seemed indifferent, and uninterested in the skaters on the ice. From time to time he took the pencil from behind his ear, made some mysterious marks and signs beside the Jelineks' name on his programme, then added a cross, until finally it was completely framed with baroque sketches. In between he read three times the part in the program where the Jelineks had been introduced to the public in five lines: 'Maria and Otto Jelinek, the young brother and sister couple from Canada, have the ambition to follow in the footsteps of their predecessors, the pair Paul and Wagner. . . .' was printed there.

"As Otto and Maria stepped on the ice, the man tapped on my shoulder: 'You know they are Czechs?' When I answered him in the affirmative, he nodded, satisfied, in agreement and in turn expressed his sympathy to me in regard to the misfortune of the German pair, Kilius and Baumler: 'They would have been "the runners-up" for sure,' he said modestly.

"Below the platform Maria and Otto made their start, three steps only, then she was floating high above him in the air, and magically slow and carefully Otto Jelinek let his sister glide down.

" 'Magnificent, fabulous,' shouted my neighbour, but he could not be heard, as the applause was louder than the music and it was evident who the 18,500 spectators wanted to have as world champions.

"Jump followed jump, with physical laws seemingly abandoned, high jumps, difficult jumps, incredibly gracious lifts, sometimes very elegant, often sportive and athletic. In between, exceedingly beautiful dancing staccatos, exactly contrary to the principle of centrifugal force, all steps marvellously in perfect unison neither ballet nor artistry, but a wonderful combination of both.

"Everything was subdued to the Jelineks: the geometry, the music, the dynamics. This splendid and miraculous routine, this genial composition and combination of ice-skated music was out of this world.

"The 18,500 spectators, who applauded during the entire five-minute program, didn't begin stamping as it ended. Neither did they shout, as so often happens after extraordinary performances; no, they clapped only. They clapped in a rage, like mad; they clapped more and more. All of them must have had blisters on their palms; the whole Ice Palace was in a deep trance, when the Jelineks took their bow.

"Otto Jelinek smiled for the first time. With a miming gesture he pointed to his sister. She graciously curtsied, smiled and sent a hand kiss into the air. Thousands thought it was for them and the echo roared back. My Czech neighbour stood and clapped. The pencil fell from his ear, he picked it up and put it in his mouth. Then he continued to applaud wildly.

"When the referees showed their marks, he wrote them down hastily, licking the pencil with his tongue and then adding the figures. Now he looked at me haughtily and said: 'We are the world champions.' Yes, he said 'we.' I heard it distinctly. I also know that the majority of the present crowd and many millions of Czech television viewers said also 'we', and meant the Jelineks."

Now the moment had come for Otto to make his champion's speech at the traditional banquet that winds up the ceremonies of the World Championships. He spoke first in English and then in Czech.

"My friends," he began, "it is my pleasant duty tonight to say thank you and farewell to Prague on behalf of all the skaters who have taken part in the world championships here this week.

"Neither word—goodbye and thanks—properly portrays our true feelings as the time to leave approaches.

"Thank you is insufficient to express our gratitude for the way the people of Prague have opened their hearts to us.

"And farewell does not explain that each of us is taking something very precious away and, I believe, leaving something just as precious here with you. That, of course, is the memory of a happy time in which the artificial boundaries which separate people were broken down and we were all friends, all forgetting

those differences which are supposed to divide us. We have seen
how slight and unimportant those differences really are. We have
seen that it is possible for a simple sport to unite people from all
corners of the earth, and having seen that it is so easily done, I
think I can promise you that the day is sure to come when we
will all be together again.

"Until then, my beloved friends, farewell and thank you."

In their eyrie on the Jacobshorn, Father and Mother and their
friends, the Haslers, watched the televising of the World Championships with taut nerves and accelerated heartbeats. For my
parents, Maria and Otto's victory was theirs, too, since so much
of themselves had gone into the preparations. Father could scarcely
contain himself.

"Champagne and caviar for everybody!" he ordered.

He and Mother and the Haslers sat in a box and were royally
served by the large staff, who also joined in the celebrations. A
storm came up during the night, a wild magnificent storm that
was both frightening and exhilarating, with snow and biting
wind. But in the morning, the storm subsided. It was calm when
the two couples came down the lift to the village of Davos.

There, they were greeted by hundreds of placards in windows:
MARIA AND OTTO WIN!

Father turned to Herr Hasler. "How did this come about?"

Herr Hasler shrugged; only later did he admit that he had
ordered them made up before the competition. Maria and Otto
were known and loved in Davos and the villagers had faith in
them.

Father beamed. He toasted his children and then he toasted
Mother, and as he told us all later, he was bewildered by the
surge of his feelings.

Maria and Otto were saying farewell to Prague. As they were
waiting for a taxi in the lobby of their hotel, a husky man with
a square face wreathed in a smile rushed up to them. He introduced himself as their original skating teacher here in Prague,
when they were stumbling beginners.

"When you were small children, I promised your mother I
would make you Czechoslovak champions. You went beyond my

wildest dreams," he added in a low voice. "You have no idea what it means to me—to all of us." His voice trembled. "Today you are not only the children of your parents. Today you are the children of our entire nation."

Epilogue

ONCE A STORM WHOSE FEROCITY IS LEGENDARY along the north shore of Lake Ontario struck down one of the finest maples gracing our lawn. Today its stump supports a round table. Here on log seats the seven members of our family have for years met and held counsel. Just as the Indians must have met, in the infant shade of this maple, in the days when the lake was *their* lake, when our lawn was *their* lawn, and missionaries were building for them the church that long years afterwards became our family home.

In winter, when the Ontario ice is far from thin, the council assembly site is transferred indoors, around a table which could have heard the wartalk of men who were forbears of the Indians. The ton-weight refectory table from England is reputed to be nearly seven centuries old.

Refectory table and maple stump—these are the repositories of the Jelinek family confidences. They have both been well thumped on occasions, as we have made fierce points in argument.

After winning the World's Championship in the land of their birth, Maria and Otto received a royal welcome in their adopted land—Canada. They put on a series of skating exhibitions throughout North America and the capitals of Europe. Later in 1962, they decided, at the behest of John H. Harris, to accept starring roles in *Ice Capades*. Father was reluctant to agree. Though he likes show-business, the idea that his children would become a part of it was somewhat inconsistent with his philosophy.

To the family's astonishment, it was Mother who encouraged Maria and Otto to take this step. She felt that the years of gruelling preparation for the glorious climax in Prague in 1962 should have a longer life cycle. Particularly because at that time Otto showed no interest in business like Frank or the academic life like Richard. He was entitled to find out whether he could achieve acceptance in the entertainment field. Maria accepted her new role of a professional skater to please Otto.

The family was at first deeply concerned with the effect of the professional life on Maria. She is wide-eyed, and vulnerable, a girl who regardless of cost remains true to her convictions. Mother greatly feared that the transition from the sheltered home to show-business might hurt and disillusion her. But Maria has adjusted beautifully. She is now completely at home with members of the *Ice Capades* company and they all share a mutual respect and affection. The code of morality backstage is more strict than in many colleges.

Both Maria and Otto are devoting their leisure to study. They are taking correspondence courses from the University of California, Maria in French and German, Otto in Business Administration.

When they retire from professional skating in the spring of 1966, Otto will no doubt find new outlets in the expanding family business. Maria plans to finish her studies at the University of Munich, majoring in languages. Her ambition is to become an interpreter for the United Nations.

Skating has brought them fame and universal acceptance.

Once they were cold frightened immigrants; now they have blossomed in the warmth of security. They have found their place in the sun, which is true of all the family.

On December 19, 1964, they won, at Lake Placid, the Professional World Pairs Skating Championship. That same day, Richard received his PhD and became Assistant Professor of Industrial Engineering at the University of Michigan.

Father and mother are often alone now, and they spend their winters in the Caribbean, spring and autumn in Europe and summers in Oakville. While in Europe, their desire to visit their relatives in Czechoslovakia is overwhelming. However, the ice there is still far too thin for them. This may change some day. Even within the last couple of years the restrictions in the countries behind the Iron Curtain are loosening, the obvious reason being their need of hard currency. When at home, our parents visit Maria and Otto at least once a month, wherever the skaters happen to be. At the peak of summer, the big sprawling house on the shore of Lake Ontario is once more alive with the family.

The Jelinek grandchildren, all four born in Canada or the United States, play on the sun dappled lawn by the pool. The family gathers around the maple tree stump. The talk is casual, but family-centered. Plans for Frank, who will soon fly to Europe or Japan on business; discussion of Richard's work in the field of hospital administration; my college grades (always a delicate subject in father's presence); a check on Maria and Otto's new tour, which will include practice sessions, costume fittings, the arrangements for publicity photographs and TV appearances.

During our vacations in Oakville, we often take out the motorboat and water ski. Our parents line up on the shore to watch. As the boat roars past our shoreline, with Maria, a nymph in a bikini, skimming the waves, we salute mother and father standing on the shore. They salute us in return. It is an old well-loved family custom, a carry over from father's military training.

It is a long way from the blood stained cobblestones of old Prague to the serene shoreline of Lake Ontario. Summers, the house is crowded with family and visitors. Guests are often amused when they hear us speak, for it is a babel of many tongues. Even back in Prague, it was our habit to use Czech, German and French all in one conversation.

We hope that we wear our experiences gracefully, the good shoring up the difficult ones, fusing them all into a whole that is perhaps in the tradition of man's exulted search for self-discovery. We have forgotten the human cruelty and remember only the human love.

Mother is holding an infant granddaughter in her arms. Maria, looking back to salute while skiing loses her balance and gets an unexpected ducking.

"Did I ever tell you," Father says, his face bright with an impish grin, "about a tumble I once had? It was on a frozen lake in the

Moravian village of Rozinka—the day I first met your mother . . ."

"And I must tell you—" Mother begins, the smile of memory glinting in her eyes.

"Yes, you must tell it," I interrupt, "and this time, I must write it."

$4⁰⁰